英語で楽しむ福岡の郷土料理
Recipes of Fukuoka

新装版 Reprinted

津田晶子 Akiko TSUDA　　**松隈紀生** Norio MATSUKUMA　　**松隈美紀** Miki MATSUGUMA
ケリー・マクドナルド Kelly MACDONALD　　**トーマス・ケイトン** Thomas CATON

海鳥社

はじめに
Preface

本書は，「昔ながらの福岡の郷土料理を楽しく学びながら，国際交流を」という目的で2009年に出版した『英語で楽しむ福岡の郷土料理』を増補したものです。昔ながらのお菓子をはじめ，ごぼう天うどんなどの人気料理のレシピを加え，福岡の「うまかもん」を幅広く紹介しています。また，だしの取り方など基本的なことも紹介していますので，参考にしてください。

本書が，英語で郷土料理を「楽しむ」きっかけづくりになれば幸いです。

最後になりましたが，本書の出版にあたり，海鳥社の田島卓氏には企画段階から大変お世話になりました。また，料理の写真撮影にあたっては，中村学園大学短期大学部食物栄養学科の仁後亮介先生，伏谷仁美先生，古川茉育先生にご協力いただきました。この場を借りて心からお礼を申し上げます。

令和という新たな時代を迎え，ここに表紙カバーを一新し，新装版としてお届けします。

This book is a revised edition of Recipes of Fukuoka, a cookbook published in 2009 with the aim of promoting international exchange through the introduction of enjoyable recipes from Fukuoka regional cuisine. The book introduces local recipes and presents cooking instructions from the making of homemade dashi stock. In this edition we have added a number of local sweets as well as popular recipes such as *Gobo-Ten Udon* (Burdock Root Tempura Udon).

It is our wish that this cookbook provide you with the opportunity to become familiar with and enjoy preparing our local dishes.

We would like to profess our sincere thanks to Mr. Suguru Tajima of Kaicho Publishing who was of tremendous help to us from the conception of this book. We would also like to thank Mr. Ryosuke Nigo, Ms. Hitomi Fushitami, and Ms. Mai Furukawa of the Nutrition Science Department of Nakamura Gakuen University Junior College for their invaluable support.

Contents 目次

■本書の使い方

① 各料理名について，エネルギー（**E**）・食物繊維（**DF**）・食塩相当量（**S**）を表示しています。
② 分量について　　計量カップ：1カップ200ccのものを使用
　　　　　　　　　　計量スプーン：大さじ15cc，小さじ5ccのものを使用

① The amount of Calories or Energy（**E**），dietary fiber（**DF**）and salt（**S**）are listed for each recipe.
② Quantities　　　1 Japanese measuring cup = 200 cc
　　　　　　　　　　1 Japanese measuring spoon: 1 TBSP = 15 cc（1/2 oz）; 1 tsp = 5 cc（1/6 oz）

だしの基本　The basics : How to prepare *dashi* stock

一番だし　一番だしには，昆布またはカツオ節だけのものと，昆布とカツオ節を一緒に使ってとるもの（混合だし）がある。一般的には，一番だしというと混合だしを指す（二番だしについても同様）。上品でクセがなく，主に吸い物用のだしとして使う。

二番だし　一番だしで使った昆布とカツオ節をさらに煮て，残った旨味をゆっくりと引き出す。主に煮物や味噌汁，炊き込みご飯用のだしとして使う。

いりこだし　昆布といりこでとるだしで，九州では主に味噌汁用のだしとして使われる。関東や関西では一般的に昆布とカツオ節の二番だしを味噌汁に使う。いりこは，イカナゴ，イワシ，アジなどの稚魚（小さなもの）を煮て干したもので，「煮干し」「だしじゃこ」とも呼ばれる。いりこの代わりにアゴ（トビウオ）を使ったものを「アゴだし」という。福岡では正月の雑煮などに使う（70ページ参照）。

＊本書では，単に「だし」という場合は二番だしを指すが，一番だしで代用してもよい。

Ichiban (primary) *dashi* stock　There are two kinds of Ichiban dashi stock: simple stock made from konbu kelp or dried bonito, or mixed stock using both of them. *Ichiban dashi* stock generally refers to the latter. It has a delicate flavor and mild taste, and is suitable for *suimono* clear soup.

Niban (secondary) *dashi* stock　Simmer used konbu kelp and dried bonito from *Ichiban dashi* to extract a good flavor. Mainly, it is used as dashi stock for boiled food, miso soup, and mixed rice.

Iriko dashi stock　This *dashi* stock is made from *konbu* kelp and *iriko*. In Kyushu, *iriko dashi* is mainly used for *miso* soup (In the Kanto and Kansai area, generally, *niban dashi* stock made from *konbu* kelp and dried bonito is used.) *Iriko* is boiled and dried young fish of sand eels, sardines, and horse mackerel, and is sometimes called *niboshi* or *dashijako*. *Agodashi* is *dashi* stock using *ago* (flying fish) instead of *iriko* and is used for *zoni* at New Years in Fukuoka (refer to p.70).

*In this book, *dashi* refers to *nibandashi* stock; however, *ichibandashi* can be used instead.

■一番だし　*Ichiban* (primary) *dashi* stock

［材料］出来上がり600cc
昆布　10g（10cm角1枚）
カツオ節　18g
水　700cc

[Ingredients]　total quantity: 600 cc
1 dried *konbu* kelp 10 cm square (10 g)
Dried bonito 18 g
700 cc water

1　昆布の表面を軽くふいて砂などをとり，700ccの水に入れて強火にかけ，沸騰直前に昆布をとり出す。

1　Wipe *konbu* kelp lightly to remove sand. Fill a pot with 700 cc water, add the *konbu* kelp, and place the pot over high heat. Just before boiling, remove the kelp from the pot.

2　カツオ節を入れてはしで軽くまぜ，20秒ぐらい煮て火を止める。

2　Add dried bonito, simmer for 20 seconds while mixing with chopsticks, and turn off the heat.

3　5分後にペーパータオルでこす。

3　Leave for 5 minutes, and strain the liquid through a paper towel.

■二番だし　*Niban* (secondary) *dashi* stock

[材料]　出来上がり600cc
一番だしの残りの昆布とカツオ節全部
カツオ節　5g
水　800cc

[Ingredients]　total quantity: 600 cc
Dried *konbu* kelp and dried bonito used for *ichiban dashi* stock
Dried bonito 5 g
800 cc water

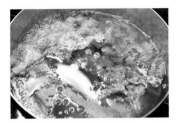

1　鍋に800ccの水と昆布, カツオ節（一番だしの残り）を入れて強火にかけ, 沸騰してきたら中火にして5分間煮る。

1　Fill a pot with 800 cc water, add the *konbu* kelp and dried bonito used for *ichiban dashi* stock, and place the pot over high heat. When the liquid comes to a boil, turn down to medium heat and simmer for 5 minutes.

2　昆布をとり出して新しいカツオ節を入れ, 20秒煮て火を止める。

2　Remove the kelp from the pot, add another 5 g of dried bonito, simmer for 20 seconds, and turn off the heat.

3　5分後にペーパータオルでこす。

3　Leave for 5 minutes, and strain the liquid through a paper towel.

■いりこだし　*Iriko dashi* stock

[材料]　出来上がり600cc
いりこ（煮干し）　25g
昆布　5g（5cm角1枚）
水　800cc

[Ingredients]　total quantity: 600 cc
Iriko (dried sardine) 25 g
1 dried *konbu* kelp 5 cm square (5 g)
800 cc water

1　いりこの頭と内臓をとり, 水, 昆布とともに鍋に入れて強火にかける。

1　Pinch away or remove entrails of *iriko* and tear into pieces. Fill a pot with cold water, add *ikiro,* and place the pot over high heat.

2　沸騰直前に昆布をとり出し, 中火でアクをすくいながら5分間煮る。

2　Just before boiling, remove the kelp from the pot. Reduce the heat to simmer for 5 minutes while removing foam, and turn off the heat.

3　ペーパータオルでこす。

3　Strain the liquid through a paper towel.

ご飯の基本　The basics: How to prepare rice

日本で一般的に食べるのはジャポニカ米で，少し粘り気がある短粒米である。米を炊く時の水加減は米容量(ccまたはカップ)の1.2倍量。すしご飯は少し固めの方がおいしいので1.1倍量にする。

In Japan, japonica rice, a rather sticky and short grain rice, is generally consumed. 1.2 cups of water per 1 cup of rice. For *sushi* rice, rather firmer rice is suitable. 1.1 cups of water per 1 cup of rice.

■米のとぎ方　How to wash rice

1　最初はたっぷりの水を加えさっとまぜてすぐに水を捨てる（米は乾燥しているので，手早くしないと，とぎ水を吸ってしまう）。
2　米と同量の水を入れ，手の平のやわらかい部分で押すようにしてとぐ。水をたっぷりと入れてとぎ水を捨てる。これを手早く3回繰り返す。
3　ザルにあげて水を切り，30分ぐらいおいて炊く。

1　As rice is dry, add a generous amount of water at first, mix lightly, and discard water right away so that it is not absorbed.
2　Add the same quantity of water as rice, and wash the rice with your hand. Pour in water to the brim, and then discard the water. Continue the procedure three times.
3　Pour the rice into a sieve, let stand for 30 minutes, and cook the rice.

■すしご飯の作り方　How to prepare *sushi* rice

［材料］4人分(1.5kg)
米　3カップ(480g)
水　660cc
昆布　10g(10cm角1枚)
みりん　15cc(大さじ1)
すし酢　酢　70cc
　　　　塩　7g
　　　　砂糖　50g

[Ingredients] 4 servings (1.5kg)
480 g rice
660 cc Water
1 dried *konbu* kelp 10 cm square (10 g)
15 cc *mirin* (sweet cooking sake)
Sushi-zu vinegar　70 cc vinegar
　　　　　　　　　　7 g salt
　　　　　　　　　　50 g sugar

1　660ccの水に昆布を入れ，1時間おいて昆布だしをとる。
2　炊飯器にといだ米と昆布だし，みりんを入れて炊く。
3　鍋に酢，塩，砂糖を入れ弱火でゆっくり溶かしてすし酢を作る（ぐらぐら沸騰させると酢の香りがなくなっておいしくない）。
4　すし桶にご飯をあけ，3のすし酢をかける。
5　木杓子を使って切るような感じでまぜ，ご飯のかたまりをほぐし，風を送って冷ます。

1　Add *konbu* kelp to 660 cc water and let stand for 60 minutes to prepare *konbu dashi* stock.
2　Place rinsed rice, the *konbu dashi* stock, and *mirin* in a rice cooker, and turn on the rice cooker.
3　[How to make *sushi* vinegar] Mix vinegar, salt, and sugar in a pan, place over low heat to dissolve gradually. (Be careful not to boil, or vinegar will lose its flavor.)
4　Transfer cooked rice (2) into the *sushi oke* bowel, pour *sushi* vinegar (3) over the rice.
5　Mix the rice by cutting across it with a fast slashing motion with a wooden spatula until the rice is smooth. Then, cool it by fanning it lightly.

すし桶は使う前に内側を洗い，布巾できれいにふいておく
Before using a *sushi oke* bowl (wooden *sushi* bowl), wipe with a wet cloth.

春
Spring

福岡城址の桜
Cherry Blossoms at Fukuoka Castle Ruins

ちらし寿司とハマグリの吸い物

Chirashizushi & Hamaguri-no-osuimono

Garnished *Sushi* & *Hamaguri* Clam Soup

ちらし寿司
Garnished *Sushi*

E 593 kcal
DF 1.3 g
S 1.4 g
（1人分　1 serving）

[材料]　4人分

すしご飯　1.5kg
　（8ページ参照）
干ししいたけ　5枚
かんぴょう（干）　10g
調味A
　だし　200cc
　しいたけ戻し汁　50cc
　砂糖　10g（大さじ1）
　濃口醤油　10cc（小さじ2）
にんじん　40g
調味B
　だし　50cc
　砂糖　2g（小さじ2/3）
　塩　ひとつまみ

冷凍エビ（長さ10cm）　5尾
調味C
　酢　50cc
　砂糖　25g（大さじ2 1/2）
炒り卵
　卵　2個
　砂糖　5g（小さじ1 1/2）
　塩　ひとつまみ
絹さや　5枚
切りのり　5g

[Ingredients] 4 servings
1.5 kg *sushi* rice
  (Refer to p.8)
5 dried *shiitake* mushrooms
10 g *kanpyo* (dried gourd shavings)
Seasoning (A)
  200 cc *dashi* stock
  50 cc *shiitake*-soaking liquid
  10 g sugar
  10 cc *koikuchi* (strong) soy sauce
40 g carrots
Seasoning (B)
  50 cc *dashi* stock
  2 g sugar
  Pinch salt
5 shrimp (frozen, 10 cm in length)
Seasoning (C)
  50 cc vinegar
  25 g sugar
Scrambled eggs
  2 eggs
  5 g sugar
  Pinch salt
5 snow peas
5 g sliced *nori* (dried laver seaweed)

[Directions]
1   Soak dried *shiitake* in water in a pot with a lid, and let stay for 5-6 hours. Rub kanpyo with salt, rinse, and boil until tender.
2   Simmer the reconstituted *shiitake* and *kanpyo* in Seasoning (A) over low heat. Remove *kanpyo* from the pan when browned and cut into round slices. Reduce the *shiitake* and slice diagonally into strips.
3   Slice carrots into 1 cm-long match-stick thin pieces, and simmer in Seasoning (B).
4   Remove the main central vein from shrimps with a bamboo skewer, and boil in lightly salted water. Remove, let soak in Seasoning (C) for 30 minutes, and cut into halves.
5   [Scrambled eggs] Beat eggs, mix with sugar and salt. Cook over medium heat, stirring with 4-5 chopsticks until the moisture has almost evaporated. Leave until other garnishes are prepared.
6   Boil snow peas in lightly salted water, drain, and cut into thin pieces.
7   Mix *kanpyo* and carrot slices with sushi rice, and garnish with other ingredients.

[作り方]
1   干ししいたけはたっぷりの水につけ, 上から皿を落とし5〜6時間おく。かんぴょうは塩10gぐらいをまぶしてもみ, 水洗いしてやわらかくなるまでゆでる。
2   しいたけ, かんぴょうの戻したものを調味Aで弱火でゆっくり煮る。かんぴょうは醤油の色が全体についたら皿にとり出し, 小口切りにする。残りの煮汁を煮つめてしいたけに照りをつけ, しいたけは大きめのそぎ切りにする。
3   にんじんは1cm長さ, マッチ軸ぐらいの太さに切り, Bの調味で煮る。
4   エビは背ワタをとり塩ゆでして調味Cに30分間つけ, 殻をむいて2つに切る。
5   炒り卵を作る。卵をといて砂糖, 塩を加える。中火にかけた鍋に卵を入れ, はし4, 5本でパラパラになるまでまぜる。
6   絹さやは塩ゆでして水にとり, 水気を切って長めのせん切りにする。
7   すしご飯にかんぴょう, にんじんをまぜ, 上に残りの具を飾る。

ハマグリの吸い物
Hamaguri Clam Soup

E 22 kcal ／ DF 0.9 g ／ S 2.2 g （1人分 1 serving）

[材料] 4人分
ハマグリ（中）　8個
昆布　10 g（10cm角1枚）
水　800cc
かいわれ　1/2束
木の芽　4枚
酒　15cc（大さじ1）
塩　4〜5 g（小さじ2/3〜1）
薄口醤油　5cc（小さじ1）

[Ingredients] 4 servings
8 clams (medium-sized)
1 dried *konbu* kelp 10 cm square (10 g)
800 cc water
1/2 radish sprouts
4 kinome (young leaves of *sansho*)
15 cc *sake*
4-5 g salt
5 cc *usukuchi* (weak) soy sauce

[作り方]
1　ハマグリは薄い塩水に5〜6時間つけて砂出しをし，殻と殻をこすりつけるようにして水で洗い，表面のぬめりをとる。
2　かいわれはさっとゆでて水にとっておく。
3　鍋に分量の水と昆布，ハマグリを入れて強火にかけ，沸騰直前に昆布をとり上げる。アクをとって弱火にし，口が開いたら酒を加え，2分間煮て醤油，塩で味を整える。
4　器に盛り，かいわれと吸い口に木の芽を添える。

[Directions]
1　Soak clams in lightly salted water for 5-6 hours to get rid of any sand. Then, wash and scrub clams with each other to clean them further.
2　Parboil radish sprouts and leave in a bowl with cold water.
3　Fill a pot with the water, kelp and clams, and place over high heat. Just before boiling, remove the kelp, skim off any foam, and reduce the heat. When the shells open, pour in sake, and simmer for two minutes, and then add the weak soy sauce and salt.
4　Ladle into individual bowls. Serve with sprouts and *kinome* as a fragrant garnish if desired.

ハマグリの話　3月3日のひな祭りは女の子の健康や成長を願って行う節句。この日にハマグリのお吸い物を食べるのは，ハマグリの殻のちょうつがいは同じ貝のものしか合わないことから，一生ひとりのご主人と添い遂げることができますようにという願いがこめられている。

Hamaguri Clams　March 3rd is the Festival of *Hina* Dolls, which wishes all girls fine health and growth. A half shell of the *hamaguri* clam can fit only the other half of the same shell, so we eat *hamaguri* clams on that day, wishing the girls a "better half for life".

あぶってかも Abbutte-kamo
Fried Damselfish

E 199 kcal ／ DF 0.5 g ／ S 1.1 g （1人分　1 serving）

［材料］4人分
スズメダイ　8尾
　（軽く塩をふって5〜6時間おいたもの）
レモンくし形切り　4個

［作り方］
塩をなじませたスズメダイを水で洗う。う
ろこのついたまま250℃のオーブントース
ターか天火でおいしそうな色がつくまで両
面を焼き，レモン汁をしぼって食べる。
＊直火焼きをした方がおいしい。

[Ingredients] 4 servings
8 *abutte-kamo* (*suzume dai*)
　or damselfish
4 lemon wedges

[Directions]
Sprinkle salt on *abutte-kamo* (no
need for scaling), and brown on both
sides in an oven-toaster or in an
oven at 250℃. Serve the fish on a
plate with lemon wedges.
*Cooking hint: Roast over a direct
flame for a more delicious fish.

あぶってかもの話　あぶってかもとは，
「焼いてそのままかむ」とか「焼いて食
べるとカモ肉のような味がする」という
ことからこの名がある。5月ぐらいにと
れるものは魚卵があり，脂がのって特に
おいしい。

Abutte-kamo (fried damselfish)
It is said that the name "*abutte-kamo*" comes from "*aburu*" (bake)
and "*kamo*" (bite), or "bake
(*aburu*) and enjoy duck (*kamo*)-
like taste". *Abutte-kamo* is particularly tasty in May, when it is rich in
fat and carrying eggs.

シロウオとつくしの卵とじ

Shirouo to Tsukushino Tamagotoji

Icy Goby and Horsetail Cooked with Eggs

E 112 kcal ／ DF 2.2 g ／ S 1.3 g （1人分　1 serving）

[材料]　4人分
シロウオ　150 g
つくし　100 g
せりまたは三つ葉　30 g
卵　2個
調味
　だし　200cc
　酒　15cc（大さじ1）
　みりん　30cc（大さじ2）
　砂糖　10 g（大さじ1）
　濃口醤油　30cc（大さじ2）

[作り方]
1　シロウオはさっと水洗いして水気を切る。つくしは,はかまをとり,水に10分間つけてアクを出し,ザルにあげて水気を切る。せりは3cm長さに切る。
2　鍋にだしと調味料を入れて強火にかけ,沸騰したらシロウオを加え,アクをとりながら2分間煮る。次につくしを加えて2分間煮て中火にし,せりを散らす。最後に溶き卵を全体に流し入れて火を止め,ふたをして1~2分蒸らし半熟に仕上げて器に盛る。

[Ingredients] 4 servings
150 g *shirouo* (Ice goby)
100 g *tsukushi* (horsetail)
30 g *seri* (Japanese parsley)
　or *mitsuba* (Japanese hornwort)
2 eggs
Seasoning
　200 cc *dashi* stock
　15 cc *sake*
　30 cc *mirin* (sweet cooking sake)
　10 g sugar
　30 cc *usukuchi* (weak) soy sauce

[Directions]
1　Rinse *shirouo* and wipe off moisture. Nip off the sheaths of *tsukushi,* soak in water for 10 minutes to remove any bitter flavor, and drain with a sieve. Cut *seri* into 3 cm lengths.
2　Pour *dashi* stock and seasoning into a pot and place over high heat. When the liquid reaches boiling point, add *shirouo* and simmer for two minutes while skimming off foam. Add the *tsukushi,* simmer for two minutes, and reduce to medium. Sprinkle on the *seri,* pour beaten egg over the surface, and turn off the heat. Cover with a lid for a few minutes to allow the egg to half-boil, and serve in a bowl.

シロウオの話　2月から4月に室見川でとれるシロウオは博多に春を告げる魚である。食べ方としては，大鉢に泳ぐシロウオをすくって，うずらの卵が入った二杯酢に入れ，ふたをして少し弱らせ，汁とともにすすりこむ「踊り食い」が有名であるが，家庭では卵とじやかき揚げ，吸い物の種にして食べる。

Shirouo Fish　*Shirouo* fish are the signal of the arrival of spring in Hakata, and are caught from February to April in the Muromigawa river. *Odorigui* eating-style at *shirouo* restaurants is very popular. To enjoy, scoop swimming *shirouo* fish from a large bowl, and put into a small bowl filled with *nihaizu* (mixture of vinegar and soy sauce) and a quail's egg (*uzurano tamago*). Cover the bowl to weaken the fish, and then sip the soup, swallowing the fish whole. At home, *shirouo* is eaten in *tamago-toji* (bound-together with egg), *kaki-age* (a deep-fried dish), and *Suimono* (clear soup).

タイ飯 *Taimeshi* E 574 kcal ／ DF 1.1 g ／ S 2.2 g （1 人分 1 serving）
Rice with Sea Bream

タイの話　日本では「くさってもタイ」といわれるほど高級な魚で，おめでたいとき
によく食べられる。玄界灘は日本でも有数のタイの産卵地で，玄界の荒波で育ったもの
は身がしまっておいしい。４月の桜の花の咲く時期のタイは，産卵前で脂がのっておい
しいので「桜ダイ」といわれる。

Tai (sea bream)　*Tai* is considered a first-class fish and is often eaten for
festive occasions in Japan. There is a proverb in Japanese, "*kusattemo tai*",
which goes "It may not be what it once was, but it is still first-class". One of
the largest spawning regions of *tai* in Japan is Genkainada; *tai* from the rough
waters here is firm and tasty. *Tai* caught during the cherry blossom season in
April (before spawning time) is called "*sakura dai*", and has an especially delicate taste.

[材料] 4人分
米　3カップ(480g)
タイ切り身(1切れ50gぐらい)　4切れ
調味A
　酒　40cc
　水　100cc
　砂糖　10g(大さじ1)
　みりん　40cc
　濃口醤油　40cc
ふき　2本
木の芽　5枚
米の水加減
　作り方2の残りの煮汁と水
　合計720cc(3.6カップ)
塩　3g(小さじ½)
切り昆布　5g

[作り方]
1　米は30分前に洗い，ザルにあげておく。
2　鍋に調味Aの酒と水を入れ，切り目を入れたタイを並べ強火にかける。沸騰してきたら砂糖，みりん，醤油を入れてふたをし，中火で3分間煮てからタイをとり出し，煮汁はこしておく。
3　ふきは塩ゆでして水にとり，皮をむき小口切りにする。
4　2の煮汁と水を合わせて720ccにし，塩と切り昆布を加え，1の洗い米を入れてご飯を炊く。
5　ご飯が炊けたら2のタイの身を入れ，10分間蒸らす。
6　5をよくまぜ合わせ器に盛り，ふきと木の芽を飾ってすすめる。

[Ingredients] 4 servings
3 cups rice (480 g)
4 sea bream fillets (50 g/each)
Seasoning
　40 cc *sake*
　100 cc water
　10 g sugar
　40 cc *mirin* (sweet cooking sake)
　40 cc *koikuchi* (strong) soy sauce
2 *fuki* (Japanese butterbur)
5 *kinome* (young leaves of *sansho*)
Liquid for cooking rice
　water+ leftover soup stock
　720 cc (3.6 cups)
3 g salt
5 g thinly sliced dried *konbu* kelp

[Directions]
1　Wash the rice 30 minutes prior to cooking and drain with a sieve.
2　Pour *sake* and water into a pot, make a cross-shape incision on one side of sea bream fillets, and simmer over high heat until boiling. Add sugar, *mirin*, and *koikuchi* soy sauce, cover the pot with a lid, and simmer over medium heat for 3 minutes. Turn off the heat, remove the fillets, and divide the solids and liquids.
3　Boil butterburs in salted water, peel, and slice into rings.
4　Add enough water to 2 (the liquid used for boiling the sea bream) to make 720 cc liquid. Add salt and thinly sliced dried *konbu* kelp to the liquid, place the rice (1) in a rice cooker with the liquid, and cook the rice.
5　Place the fish meat (2) on the rice and allow the boiled rice to settle for 10 minutes.
6　Open the cover of the rice cooker, mix the rice well and serve in individual bowls with butterburs and *kinome*.

タイのあら炊き *Tai-no-aradaki*

Simmered Sea Bream

E 337 kcal ／ DF 2.9 g ／ S 3.0 g （1人分　1 serving）

[材料] 4人分
タイ　1尾(700g)
　（またはタイのあら）
ごぼう（中）　180g
煮汁
　酒　80cc
　みりん　80cc
　濃口醤油　80cc
　水　160cc
　砂糖　36g（大さじ4）
木の芽　4枚
絹さや　12枚

[Ingredients] 4 servings
1 sea bream (700 g)
　(or bony parts of the fish)
180 g burdock roots
Simmering liquid
　80 cc *sake*
　80 cc *mirin* (sweet cooking sake)
　80 cc *koikuchi* (strong) soy sauce
　160 cc water
　36 g sugar
4 *kinome* (young leaves of *sansho*)
12 snow peas

[作り方]
1　タイはうろこ，えら，内臓をとり，水で洗う。頭を切り落とし，身を2枚におろし，6切れにする。頭は縦に割り，熱湯に入れすぐ水にとり，残っているうろこをとりのぞく。
2　ごぼうはよく洗い，5cm長さに切り，太い部分は縦4つ割りにし，水につけてアクを抜く。絹さやはすじをとり，さっとゆでる。
3　鍋にごぼうを並べ，上にタイをおいて酒と水を入れ，落としぶたをして煮る。タイの目玉が白くなったらみりんと砂糖を加えて3分の1の量まで煮つめ，醤油を2，3回に分けて入れ強火にし，煮汁をかけながら照りよく煮る。
4　器に盛り，ごぼうと絹さやを手前に添え，煮汁をかけて木の芽を飾る。

[Directions]
1　Scale, clear and wash the sea bream. Cut off the head and slice the fish into two pieces lengthwise, and then slice into 6 fillets. Slice the fish head lengthwise, boil in hot water, and rinse to remove the scales.
2　Wash the burdock roots, and cut into 5 cm pieces. Divide the thick parts into 4 pieces. Soak in water to remove any harsh taste. Remove strings from snow peas, and parboil.
3　Put the burdock roots into a pan, place the fish on top, pour in *sake* and water, cover with a drop lid, and simmer. When the eyeballs turn white, add *mirin* and sugar, and simmer down until reduced to one-third. Add soy sauce in small quantities, turn up the heat, and spoon the liquid over the fish and burdock roots while simmering.
4　Arrange the burdock roots and snow peas in front of the fish, and pour on the simmering liquid. Add *kinome* as garnish.

あら炊きの話　魚の頭や中骨の部分を「魚のあら」という。本書のレシピでは身も使ったが，もともとは，身の部分は刺身や焼き物に料理し，残ったあらを少し甘めに味つけして煮たものを「あら炊き」という。

Aradaki　"*Sakana-no-Ara*" means the bony parts of fish, including the head bones and spine. After using the fish meat for *sashimi* or baked fish, *ara* can be used for *Aradaki,* a boiled dish with a little sweetening. This recipe uses both fish meat and *ara.*

おきゅうと *Okyuto*

Jellied Seaweed

E 6 kcal／DF 1.1 g／S 0.2 g （1人分　1 serving）

[材料] 1人分
おきゅうと　1枚
カツオ節　少々
白ごま　少々
濃口醬油　少々

[作り方]
1　おきゅうとは，さっと水洗いして 5 mm 幅に切る。
2　器におきゅうとを盛り，カツオ節，炒りごまを手でひねり上にかけ，醬油をかけていただく。

[Ingredients] 1 serving
1 okyuto
Dried bonito flakes
White sesame
Koikuchi (strong) soy
　sauce

[Directions]
1　Rinse *okyuto* and slice into 5 mm pieces.
2　Arrange *okyuto* on a plate. Twist up dried bonito flakes and sesame and sprinkle over the *okyuto*. Pour on soy sauce to serve.

おきゅうとの話　ひと昔前まで，博多の町では，早朝に「おきゅうとーおきゅうとー」のふれ声のおきゅうと売りが見られた。語源としては沖独活（おきうど。沖でとれるウド）とか，昔飢饉のとき非常食として多くの命を救ったことから「救人（きゅうと）」といわれるようになったという説もある。主原料はえごのりやいぎす，てんぐさなどの海藻で，これをきれいに洗って干し，熱湯の中に酢少々を加えて 1 時間ぐらい煮てドロドロにとかし，流し箱に流し固めて作る。おきゅうとは食物繊維やミネラルが多く，健康のためにも毎日食べることをおすすめしたい。

Okyuto　*Okyuto* vendors used to walk around the streets of Hakata in the morning, shouting "Okyu-to, Okyu-to". The word Okyuto is said to be derived from the combination of *oki* (offshore) and *udo* (*udo* plants). Another story suggests *okyuto* was an emergency food during famine, helping a lot of people survive. The name is believed to be the combination of *kyu* (save) and *hito* (people). The main raw materials of *okyuto* are marine plants, including *egonori, igisu,* and *tengusa*. To make *okyuto,* wash and dry the marine plants, boil in hot water with a little vinegar for around one hour so as to reduce to a jelly, and pour into a pan. *Okyuto* is rich in dietary fiber and minerals. Those who want to stay healthy are encouraged to eat *okyuto* every day.

高菜漬け油炒め　*Takanazuke, abura-itame*
Fried *Takana* Pickles

E 31 kcal ／ DF 0.8 g ／ S 0.7 g （1人分　1 serving）

[材料]　1人分
高菜漬け　50g
白ごま　3g（小さじ1）
一味唐辛子　少々
ごま油　10cc（小さじ2）

[Ingredients]　1 serving
50 g *takanazuke* pickles
3 g white sesame
Ichimi-tougarashi pepper
10 cc sesame oil

[作り方]
1　高菜漬けを水洗いして水気をしぼり小口切りにする。
2　鍋にごま油を熱し1の高菜を入れて炒め，白ごま，一味唐辛子を加える。

[Directions]
1　Wash *takanazuke* pickles, drain, and cut into pieces.
2　Heat a pan with sesame oil, and stir 1 in the pan. To serve, sprinkle on sesame and ichimi pepper.

高菜漬けの話　筑後地方一帯で作られる三池高菜は，葉が広くきれいな緑色に漬け上がるので，高菜おむすびや高菜チャーハンに使われる。昔は，各家庭で1年分漬けられ，古くなると酸味が強くなってくるので油炒めにして食べた。おいしく食べるための工夫である。

Takanazuke Miike-Takana, produced in the area of Chikugo, is used for *takana omusubi* rice-balls and *takana* fried rice, as the leaves are rather large and turn vivid green when they are pickled. Each household used to pickle a year's worth of *takana* at a time and preserve it. The dish, "fried *tanaka* pickles" was thought up to enjoy the pickles that turned sour over the year.

博多の朝ご飯の一例
Hakata-style breakfast

1 おきゅうと　Jellied Seaweed
2 明太入り卵焼き　Rolled Egg with *Mentai*
3 白ご飯　White Rice
4 高菜漬け油炒め　Fried *Takana* Pickles
5 貝汁（アサリの味噌汁）　*Kaijiru Miso* Soup

Column

食材を買いに街に出かけよう

いつものスーパーに飽きたら，たまには食材を買いに街に出かけよう。

天気がいい日のおすすめは，西新の商店街に所狭しと店を並べる「リヤカー部隊」だ。花や野菜，果物はもちろん，手づくりのもち，漬物，ゆずごしょうなどを売る店もある。春になれば，春の七草やつくし，アサリが並ぶ。季節感たっぷりの旬の食材が手に入るはず。調理方法がわからなければ，思い切って，リヤカーのおばちゃんに尋ねてみよう。飾らないのが庶民の町・西新なのだから。

本格的な魚好きなら「柳橋連合市場」へ。鮮魚だけでなく，あごだし，明太子，かまぼこなどの地元の魚介加工品を扱う専門店もある。天神からバスで10分足らずの場所にある「博多の台所」で，地元の食文化に触れてみたい。

Let's Go Hunting for Locally Produced Fukuoka Food!

If you feel bored buying at supermarkets close to your home, why don't you go out to seek locally-produced foods once in a while?

Weather permitting, go and check out "*Rear-Car Butai*" street-vendors with their two-wheeled carts, crammed along the *Nishijin Shotengai* shop street.

They sell not only raw agricultural goods, such as flowers, vegetables and fruits, but also homemade *mochi* rice cakes, pickles and *yuzu gosho* pepper. In spring, *Haru-no-nanakusa* herbs, horsetail, and little neck clams are sold at these vendors. You can surely get delicacies of the season from "*Rear-Car Butai*". When you find something unfamiliar, don't hesitate to ask the *Rear-Car* vendor owners for cooking ideas, as Nishijin is a town full of local color, and the local people are approachable with their easy manners.

For authentic seafood, the *Yanagi-bashi rengo ichiba* market is a must, with its fresh fish as well as processed fishery products, such as *agodashi, mentaiko* and *kamaboko*. A less than 10 minute-bus ride from Tenjin will take you to this market. Also called "*Hakata-no-daidokoro* (Hakata's Kitchen)", it is a place where you can experience local food culture.

夏
Summer

糸島の海
Itoshima Beach

アジの博多おし *Aji-no-Hakata-oshi*
Hakata-style Pressed Mackerel *Sushi*

E 266 kcal ／ DF 0.8 g ／ S 1.1 g （1人分　1 serving）

[材料] 4人分
アジ三枚おろし（刺身用）　3尾分
塩　100g
甘酢　酢　200cc
　　　砂糖　100g
　　　赤唐辛子　1本
だいこん　70g
にんじん　70g
（すし飯を使う場合）
　すし飯　200g
　　（8ページ参照）
　しその葉　5枚
　しょうが　10g

[作り方]
1　アジの身の両面に塩をぬりつけるようにして，冷蔵庫で30分間しめる。
2　1の塩を水で洗い落として水気をふき，甘酢に10分間つける。次に骨抜きで中骨をとり，頭の方から皮をはぎ，横半分に切る。
3　だいこん，にんじんは薄切りにして軽く塩をふり，しんなりとしたら水洗いして甘酢に10分間つける。
4　抜き型または深めの四角い器にラップをしいて2のアジ，だいこん，アジ，にんじん，アジの順に重ね，ラップでまいて皿を2，3枚のせる。10分後にとり出し，ひと口大に切り器に盛る。
＊にんじん，だいこんの代わりに，すし飯，しそ，しょうがを使ってもよい。

[Ingredients] 4 servings
3 fillets *aji* (horse mackerel)
100 g salt
Sugared vinegar
　200 cc vinegar
　100 g sugar
　1 red chilli
70 g radishes
70 g carrots
(For variation)
　200 g *sushi* rice (Refer to p.8)
　5 *shiso* (Japanese perilla) leaves
　10 g sliced ginger

[Directions]
1　Spread salt on both sides of fillets, and refrigerate for 30 minutes.
2　Rinse the fillets to wash off the salt, wipe off moisture, and soak in sugared vinegar for 10 minutes. Pick out any small belly bones, peel the skin from the head with tweezers, and cut into half crosswise.
3　Slice radishes and carrots into thin pieces, sprinkle salt, and let it stand. Then, rinse and soak in sugared vinegar for 10 minutes.
4　Spread plastic wrap/cling film on a cutting board or rectangular dish, and lay fillets (2) on top. Lay radishes, fillets and carrots, on top of one another, add another layer of fillets, and spread plastic wrap on top. Place a few dishes on top as a weight and let stay for 10 minutes. Unwrap, cut into bite-sized pieces, and serve.
*Variation: *Sushi* rice, *shiso* leaves and ginger slices can be used instead of fillets, radishes and carrots.

博多おしの話　切り口が縞目（しまめ）模様になり博多帯の柄に似ているため「博多」という名がつけられた。他にも「高野豆腐とエビの博多蒸し」や「キャベツと豚肉の博多」などがある。

Hakata-oshi　The stripe of the cut edge resembles the pattern of a *Hakata-obi* belt, so this dish is called "*Hakata Oshi*" (Hakata Press). "Hakata-style of *koya tofu* and shrimps" and "Cabbage and pork à la Hakata" are variations of *Hakata-oshi*.

サザエご飯 *Sazae Gohan*

Cooked Rice with Turban Shells

E 471 kcal ／ DF 2.0 g ／ S 2.5 g （1人分　1 serving）

[材料] 4人分
米　3カップ（480g）
サザエ（大）　3個
にんじん　50g
ごぼう　30g
春菊　50g
調味A
　　だし　150cc
　　薄口醬油　30cc（大さじ2）
　　砂糖　10g（大さじ1）
　　酒　30cc（大さじ2）
4の煮汁＋だし　合計3.6カップ
塩　3g（小さじ½）

[作り方]
1　米は炊く30分前に洗いザルにあげておく。にんじん，ごぼうは荒みじんに切る。
2　サザエは殻をよく洗い，鍋にサザエが半分つかるぐらいの水を入れ，強火にかける。沸騰して3分間ゆでたら身をとり出し，固い部分を薄切りにする。下の方のやわらかい部分は1cm幅に切る。
3　鍋に調味A，にんじん，ごぼうを入れ1分間煮て，2のサザエを加えてさらに1分間煮る。
4　3をアミでこし，煮汁はとっておく。
5　4の煮汁にだしを加え3.6カップにし，塩を加え1の米と4の具を入れて炊く。
6　ご飯が炊き上がったらゆがいた春菊の小口切りを加えてよくまぜ，器に盛る。

[Ingredients]　4 servings
480 g rice
3 *sazae* (large-sized turban shells)
50 g carrots
30 g burdock roots
50 g *shungiku* (chrysanthemum leaves)
Seasoning (A)
　150 cc *dashi* stock
　30 cc *usukuchi* (weak) soy sauce
　10 g sugar
　30 cc *sake*
Liquid 4 + *dashi* stock (total 3.6 cups)
3 g salt

[Directions]
1　Wash rice, drain with a sieve, and let stand for 30 minutes. Chop carrots and burdock roots.
2　Wash *sazae* to clean. Place in a pan, pouring in just enough water to cover the *sazae,* and cook over high heat. Simmer for 3 minutes after boiling, take out the shellfish meat, and slice up the hard parts of the meat. Cut the soft parts into 1 cm slices.
3　Place Seasoning (A) in the pan, add carrots and burdock roots, and simmer for 1 minute. Then, add sazae (2) and simmer for 1 minute.
4　Drain 3 with a sieve and keep the liquid used for simmering.
5　Add *dashi* stock to this liquid (4) to make 720cc in total.　Add salt to the liquid, placing the rice (1) and the ingredients (4) in the rice cooker, and switch on the cooker.
6　When cooked, open the cover of the rice cooker, add sliced shungiku leaves, mix the rice well, and serve in individual bowls.

サザエご飯の話　サザエご飯は志賀島でよく作られる炊き込みご飯である。海に近い所では，アワビご飯，サワラご飯など，魚介類を使った炊き込みご飯が多い。

Sazae gohan　*Sazae gohan* is a kind of "*Takikomi gohan*", cooked rice with various ingredients, often cooked on Shikanoshima island. In the coastal areas in Fukuoka, they serve local "*Takikomi gohan*" using seafood such as *awabi* (abalone) or *sawara* (Spanish mackerel).

柳川鍋 *Yanagawa nabe*
Yanagawa-style *Nabe*

E 214 kcal ／ DF 2.9 g ／ S 0.7 g
（1 人分　1 serving）

[材料] 4人分
アナゴ（開いたもの）　2尾分（280 g）
ごぼう　150 g
生しいたけ　4枚
三つ葉　15 g
卵　4個
粉さんしょう　少々
あわせ調味料　だし　280cc
　　　　　　　みりん　70cc
　　　　　　　薄口醤油　70cc
　　　　　　　砂糖　15 g（大さじ 1 1/2）

[作り方]
1　開いたアナゴは 2 つに切り，背びれの部分をとりのぞく。まな板に皮を上にしておき，熱湯をかけ，包丁の刃で表面のぬめりをこそげとり，2 cm幅，6 cm長さのななめ切りにする。
2　ごぼうはささがきにして水にさらし，生しいたけは薄切り，三つ葉は 3 cm長さに切る。
3　あわせ調味料を鍋に入れ火にかけて砂糖をとかしておく。
4　浅い土鍋またはフライパンにごぼう，生しいたけを全体にしき，穴子を放射状に並べ，3 を材料がつかるぐらい入れ強火にかける。
5　沸騰してごぼうとアナゴに火が通ったら卵をといて全体にかけ三つ葉を散らす。ふたをして卵が半熟になったら出来上がり。好みで粉さんしょうをふって食べる。

柳川鍋の話　名前の由来は福岡県柳川産の土鍋を用いたからとも，江戸時代に「柳川」という屋号の店で初めて出されたからともいわれる。本来はドジョウという川魚を使うが，アナゴやウナギ，牛肉などでも作られる。ごぼうを使うことで魚の生臭みを感じさせず，おいしく食べることができる。

Yanagawa-nabe　There are several stories behind the name "*Yanagawa-nabe*". Some claim that this dish was cooked in earthen pots made in Yanagawa City, Fukuoka prefecture, while others say that in the Edo-era it was served for the first time at a restaurant named "*Yanagawa*". Basically, we use loach, a kind of freshwater fish, for this dish. *Anago* or sea eel, *unagi* or eel, or beef can be used instead of loach. Adding burdock roots disguises the strong smell of the fish and makes the dish more enjoyable.

[Ingredients] 4 servings
280 g sea eel (2 fillets)
150 g burdock roots
4 *shiitake* mushrooms
15 g *mitsuba* (Japanese hornwort)
4 eggs
Powdered *sansho* (Japanese pepper)
Mixed seasoning
  280 cc *dashi* stock
  70 cc *mirin* (sweet cooking *sake*)
  70 cc *usukuchi* (weak) soy sauce
  15 g sugar

[Directions]

1   Slice the halved-eel into two pieces crosswise and remove the dorsal fins. Place the fillets on a cutting board with the skin side up, pour on hot water, scrape the slack (sticky surface) with the blade of a kitchen knife, and cut diagonally into pieces of 2 cm width, 6 cm length.

2   Shave the burdock roots with a knife and soak in water. Slice *shiitake* mushrooms into thin pieces. Cut *mitsuba* into 3 cm pieces.

3   Pour the mixed seasoning into a pot and simmer until the sugar has dissolved.

4   Spread the burdock roots and mushrooms over the bottom of a flat earthen pot or frying pan, place the fillets in a radial pattern on top, and pour in enough 3 to cover the ingredients. Cook over high heat.

5   When the liquid reaches a boil, and when the burdock roots and fillets are well-cooked, pour over the beaten eggs, sprinkle on *mitsuba,* and cover with a lid. Wait until the egg is half-boiled. If desired, sprinkle on powdered *sansho*.

ささがきごぼう *Sasagaki gobo*
Burdock roots skin shaving

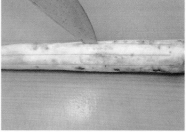

ごぼうの皮を包丁の背で軽くこそぎとり，中心の所まで6mm幅に切り目を入れ，削るようにして切って水にとる。
Scrape off the burdock root skin using the back of a knife, and make an incision about 6 mm deep at one end. Shave from that end as if you were sharpening a pencil and soak in water.

棒ダラの甘辛煮（盆タラ）

Boudara no Amakara-ni (Bon Tara)

Sweet and Salty Codfish

E 590 kcal ／ DF 3.0 g ／ S 7.1 g （1人分　1 serving）

棒ダラの甘辛煮の話　タラの身を干したものを棒ダラと呼び，タラのエラと内臓部分を干したものをタラワタと呼ぶ。このタラワタも甘辛く煮て，そうめんとともに食べる。棒ダラの甘辛煮やタラワタ煮は，海魚が手に入りにくい山間部や農村部のお盆のごちそうだった。昔からこの時期の女性たちは，仏様に供える料理やお客様の接待などで大変忙しかった。15日の夕方，送り火で仏様が帰った後に女性たちが集まってこの料理を食べ，今で言う"打ち上げ"を行ったと，あるおばあさんが話してくれた。

[材料] 4人分
棒ダラ（干） 160g
水 棒ダラがつかるくらい
酒 50cc
しょうが（せん切り） 10g
細切り昆布 10g
ざらめ 80g
濃口醤油 50cc
板ゼラチン 3g
そうめん 4束

[Ingredients] 4 servings
160 g dried codfish
Water (enough to soak the cod)
50 cc *sake*
10 g sliced ginger
10 g *konbu* kelp (finely sliced)
80 g granulated sugar
50 cc *koikuchi* (strong) soy sauce
3 g gelatin leaf
4 bunches *somen* (fine wheat) noodles

[作り方]
1 棒ダラは，たっぷりの水に5～6時間つけて戻す（2回くらい水を替えるとよい）。
2 板ゼラチンは，たっぷりの水に20分つけて戻す。
3 1を7cm長さに切り鍋に入れ，棒ダラがつかる程度の水と酒，しょうが，昆布を入れ強火にかける。
4 3が沸騰してきたら弱火にして時々アクをすくい，落としぶたをして20分間煮る。次にざらめ，醤油を入れてさらに30分間煮て，板ゼラチンを加える。
5 煮汁が少なくなってきたら中火にして棒ダラに煮汁をかけ，つやが出てきたら出来上がり。
6 そうめんを沸騰した湯で1分間ゆでて水にとり，軽くもみ洗いしてザルにとる。
7 棒ダラを器に盛り煮汁をかけ，手前にそうめんを飾る。

[Directions]
1 Reconstitute the cod by soaking 5-6 hrs in water, changing the water twice.
2 Reconstitute the gelatin by soaking in water for 20 mins.
3 Cut 1 into 7 cm strips and put into a pot over high heat with ginger, kelp, *sake*, cod, and enough water to cover.
4 When 3 comes to a boil, reduce heat to low and remove any foam. Cover with a drop lid, and simmer for 20 mins. Add granulated sugar and soy sauce, simmer for 30 mins, and add gelatin.
5 When little soup remains, reduce to medium heat and spoon over the cod. When the soup takes on a glossy sheen, remove from heat.
6 Add the *somen* to boiling water. Boil for 1 min, lightly rinse in cold water, and drain with a sieve.
7 Place the cod in a dish, spoon on the soup, and arrange the *somen* around the front of the cod.

Sweet and Salty Codfish Codfish which has been dried is called "*boudara*". Dried gills and entrails are known as "*tarawata*". This *tarawata* is also simmered in a sweet and salty soup and eaten with *somen* noodles. In mountainous districts and farming areas where ocean fish was hard to come by, *Boudara-ni* and *Tarawata-ni* were regarded as a feast and eaten during *Obon* holidays. Women at this time were extremely busy preparing food for the Buddhist altar and for guests, so after sending off the spirits of their ancestors with a ceremonial bonfire, they gathered to eat this dish in a celebration much like we now call *uchiage* (a party to celebrate the successful completion of something).

あちゃら漬け *Achara zuke*

Achara-zuke Pickles   E 203 kcal ／ DF 8.9 g ／ S 0.4 g（1人分　1 serving）

あちゃら漬けの話　夏の料理で特にお盆に作られる。ポルトガル語で漬物を意味する「アチャール」に由来する。にんじんや花ふを使うところもあり，材料は縁起が良いとされる奇数種類を使う。

Achara-zuke pickles　*Achara-zuke* pickles are summer pickles, mainly pickled during the *O-Bon* holidays. The name comes from the Portuguese word "*achar*" for pickles. Some people use carrots or *hanafu,* a flower-shaped wheat gluten cake. Odd numbers are considered lucky in Japan, so 7 types of pickles are presented here.

[材料] 4人分
れんこん　150g
ごぼう　100g
白うり　150g
ずいき（はすいもの葉柄）　100g
かんぴょう（干）　20g
きくらげ（干）　20g
昆布　20g
あちゃら酢　酢　200cc
　　　　　砂糖　120g
　　　　　だし　50cc
　　　　　赤唐辛子　1本

[Ingredients] 4 servings
150 g lotus root
100 g burdock roots
150 g *shirouri* melon
100 g *zuiki/imogara* (roots of dried taro)
20 g *kanpyo* (dried gourd shavings)
20 g dried *kikurage* (Jew's ear fungus)
20 g *konbu* kelp
Achara-su vinegar　　200 cc vinegar
　　　　　　　　　　120 g sugar
　　　　　　　　　　50 cc *dashi* stock
　　　　　　　　　　1 red chilli pepper

[作り方]
1　赤唐辛子は種をとり輪切りにする。
2　あちゃら酢を作る。鍋に酢，砂糖，だしを入れて火にかけ砂糖をとかし，火を止めて1を加え冷ましておく。
3　れんこんは皮をむき，3mm厚さの半月切りにして水にさらし，ゆでる。
4　ごぼうは表面の黒皮をこそぎとり4cm長さに切り，太い部分は4つ割り，細い部分は2つ割りにして水にさらし，ゆでる。
5　白うりはタテ半分に切って種をとり薄切りにし，しんなりとするまで塩もみし，水洗いして水気をしぼる。
6　ずいきは手で皮をむき親指くらいの太さに切り，さっとゆでて水にとり水気をしぼる。
7　かんぴょうは塩もみをして水洗いし，ツメで押して形がつくぐらいまでゆでて水にとり，水気をしぼり5cm長さに切って結んでおく。
8　きくらげはゆがいて戻し，石づきをとりひと口大に切っておく。
9　結び昆布を作る。昆布をぬれ布巾にはさんでやわらかくし，1cm幅，6cm長さにハサミで切り結ぶ。
10　あちゃら酢が冷めたら3～9の材料を1時間くらい漬け込み器に盛る。

[Directions]
1　Remove seeds from red chilli, and slice finely.
2　[How to make *achara-su* vinegar] Pour vinegar, sugar and *dashi* stock into a pan, and heat until the sugar has dissolved. Add 1, and leave to cool.
3　Remove the skin of the lotus root, cut into 3 mm half-moon slices, soak in water, and boil.
4　Scrape the black peel off the burdock roots, and cut into 4 cm pieces. Split thick parts into four, and thin parts into two. Rinse and boil.
5　Cut *shirouri* into halves lengthwise, remove seeds, and slice thinly. Rub with salt, rinse, and squeeze out excess moisture.
6　Remove the skin of *zuiki/imogara* by hand, cut into thumb-sized pieces, and parboil. Soak in water, and squeeze out any excess moisture.
7　Rub *kanpyo* with salt, rinse, and boil until soft enough to leave nail marks when pinched. Soak in water, and squeeze out any excess moisture. Cut into 5 cm slices, and make a knot.
8　Parboil *kikurage* to reconstitute, cut away any root clusters, and slice into bite-sized pieces.
9　[How to make *musubi konbu*] Sandwich soft parts of dried *konbu* kelp between a wet cloth to reconstitute, cut into pieces 1 cm wide, 6 cm long with scissors, and make a knot.
10　When the vinegar has cooled, pickle 3 - 9 in the vinegar for around 1 hour, and then serve in dishes.

山ごんにゃくの刺身 *Yama gonnyaku-no-sashimi*

Konnyaku Salad

E 9.2 kcal ／ DF 3.6 g ／ S 0.1 g （1 人分　1 serving）

こんにゃくの刺身の話　お盆のときの料理や精進料理では魚の刺身が食べられないので，こんにゃくを刺身風にして出す。八女や筑後地方，その他の山間部では手づくりのおいしいこんにゃくが作られる。

Konnyaku-no-Sashimi　The Japanese cannot eat *sashimi* (raw fish) with *shojin ryori* (Buddhist vegetarian dishes) or during the Obon holidays, so *sashimi*-like sliced *konnyaku* (devil's tongue) is sometimes served. In the mountainous areas of Japan such as the Yame and Chikugo-areas, delicate hand-made *konnyaku* is produced.

[材料] 4人分
山ごんにゃく 1丁
　（山間部の農家で作られる手
　づくりこんにゃく）
きゅうり 1本
しその葉 4枚
ゆずごしょう 適量
濃口醤油 適量

[Ingredients] 4 servings
1 *yama gonnyaku*
　(home-made devil's tongue)
1 cucumber
4 *shiso* (Japanese perilla)
Yuzu gosho pepper
Koikuchi (strong) soy sauce

[作り方]
1　山ごんにゃくは表面を塩でも
み，水洗いして20分間ゆで，ザル
にとり冷めたら冷蔵庫に入れてさ
らに冷やす。
2　きゅうりは細切りにして氷水
につけ，けんにする。
3　1をさざ波切り（包丁の刃を
を立てたり寝かせたりして表面に
飾りをつける）にし，しその葉を
そえて刺身のように盛りつけ，ゆ
ずごしょうと醤油をつけて食べる。
＊フグ造り（フグの刺身のように
薄く切る）にして酢味噌をつけて
食べてもおいしい。

[Directions]
1　Rub the surface of home-made devil's tongue with salt, and wash off. Boil for 20 minutes, drain with a sieve to allow to cool, arrange on a plate, and chill in the refrigerator.
2　Slice cucumber thinly, and allow to soak in iced water.
3　Shave the devil's tongue into thin wave-like shapes using the edge of a knife. Serve the shaved devil's tongue like *sashimi* with *yuzu gosho* pepper, and soy sauce.
*Variation: *Konnyaku* can also be served like *fugu-zukuri sashimi* (thinly sliced globefish), with *sumiso* (vinegar bean paste).

ゆずごしょうの話　山間部の農家では緑色のゆずの皮と緑色のこしょうをすりつぶして，香りが良くピリッとしたゆずごしょうが作られる。福岡では鍋物，味噌汁，漬物，うどんなどに辛味の材料として使われる。

Yuzu Gosho Farming families in mountainous areas make *yuzu gosho,* a piquant pepper with aroma, by grinding green-colored *yuzu* skin and pepper. In Fukuoka, *yuzu gosho* is used as a spice in *nabe* dishes, *miso* soups, pickles, and *udon* noodles.

Column

ヘルシーな福岡の郷土料理

外国人の中には，市販のブイヨンやだしをあまり使わない人も多いため，本書では，昆布とカツオ節，いりこのだしや，チキンスープのとり方を紹介している。

玄界灘の海の幸や野菜をふんだんに使う福岡の郷土料理は，カロリーが低く，ヘルシーな食生活を志向する人にはおすすめだ。乳製品や赤身の肉，ラードなどをほとんど使わないため，ベジタリアンでも楽しめるものが多い。特にベジタリアンやムスリム（イスラム教徒）の方に料理を振る舞う際には，念のためレシピの材料の1つひとつを英語で示し，食べられないものが入っていないか確認するといいだろう。

Fukuoka's Healthy Regional Cuisine

The commercially sold bouillon or dashi soup stock commonly available in Japan may be unfamiliar for some foreigners, so they should appreciate the dishes made from konbu kelp and dried bonito, dried sardine, or chicken stock which are introduced in this cookery book.

Fukuoka's regional cuisine is low in calories, full of vegetables, and abundant in fish and seafood from the Ariake Sea, so it is particularly recommended for those engaging in healthy lifestyles. Dairy products, red meat and lard are rarely used, so there are a number of dishes that can also be enjoyed by vegetarians. Those with dietary restrictions such as vegetarians or Muslims should check the list of ingredients in the recipes carefully to make sure the dishes are suitable for their diet.

秋
Autumn

秋月の紅葉
Autumn Colors in Akizuki

ごまサバ茶漬け *Gomasaba Chazuke*
Boiled Rice with Sesame-flavored Mackerel

E 215 kcal ／ DF 1.0 g ／ S 1.9 g （1 人分　1 serving）

[材料] 4人分
マサバ切り身（刺身用） 300 g
ごま醬油
　炒りごま　30 g（大さじ 3 ）
　砂糖　10 g（大さじ 1 ）
　濃口醬油　45cc（大さじ 3 ）
　だし　15cc（大さじ 1 ）
しその葉　6 枚
わさび　少々
ご飯　適量
番茶　適量

[Ingredients] 4 servings
300 g half-sliced mackerel (for *sashimi*)
Goma-joyu (sesame soy sauce)
　30 g *irigoma* (roasted sesame)
　10 g sugar
　45 cc *koikuchi* (strong) soy sauce
　15 cc *dashi* stock
6 *shiso* (Japanese perilla)
Wasabi (Japanese horseradish)
Cooked rice
Bancha tea (coarse green tea)

[作り方]
1　3 枚におろしたサバの身は頭の方から薄皮をとり，腹骨と小骨をとりのぞき 3 ㎜厚さのそぎ切りにする。
2　すり鉢にごまを入れ半ずりにし，残りの調味料を加え，1 のサバを10分くらいつけこむ。
3　アツアツのご飯の上に 2 のごまサバをおき，つけ汁を15ccかけ，しその葉のせん切りをのせてわさびをそえ，熱い番茶をかけてすすめる。
＊茶漬けにしないで，ごまサバとして食べてもよい。

[Directions]
1　Divide each fish into three fillets. Remove the skin from the head, and get rid of belly bones and other small bones. Slice the fish diagonally into 3 mm pieces.
2　Roughly-grind some sesame in a mortar, and add sugar, *koikuchi* (strong) soy sauce and *dashi* stock to make *goma joyu* (sesame soy) sauce. Soak 1 in the sauce for 10 minutes.
3　Place 2 (*Gomasaba*) on the cooked rice, pour on *goma joyu* sauce (15 cc), add thinly sliced *shiso* and *wasabi,* and pour on *bancha* tea to serve.
*Variation: The dish can also be enjoyed as "*gomasaba*", without the tea.

ごまサバの話　福岡の平野部は漁場と町との距離が近いため，新鮮な魚が食べられる。関東では，サバは酢でしめた「しめサバ」しか食べないが，福岡では生のサバを刺身として食べる習慣がある。ごまサバの正式な料理名は「サバのごま醬油」という。タイ，アジなどでも作られる。

Gomasaba　Thanks to the rather short distance between the fishing grounds and the city, really fresh fish can be eaten in Fukuoka. While people in Kanto eat only *shimesaba,* or vinegared mackerel, Fukuokans can often eat mackerel raw. The official recipe name of *Gomasaba* is "*Saba-no-Goma-joyu*". *Tai* (sea bream) or *aji* (horse mackerel) can be used instead of *saba*.

カマスの姿鮨 *Kamasu-no-Sugatazushi*
Barracuda Stuffed with *Sushi* Rice

E 471 kcal／DF 0.7 g／S 3.0 g　（1人分　1 serving）

カマスの姿鮨の話　昔は，とれたてのカマスやサバを開き，塩をまぶしたものを行商の人が山間部の村に売りにきていた。ちょうど2，3時間たってほどよく身がしまっているので，これを姿鮨にして，祭りやお祝いのときに食べた。当時の山間部の人々にとってはごちそうであった。

Kamasu-no-Sugatazushi　Filleted and salted fresh *kamasu* (barracuda) and *saba* (mackerel) have long been peddled in villages and over the mountains. Typically when they were bought, a few hours had already passed since processing. Villagers cooked *Sugata-zushi* with *kamasu* and *saba* for festivals and celebrations. For the villagers and people living in the mountains, *sugata-zushi* was regarded as a feast.

40

[材料] 4人分
新鮮なカマス（1尾300～400ｇ）
　　2尾
塩　120ｇ
甘酢
　酢　200cc
　砂糖　100ｇ
　赤唐辛子　1本
すし飯　700ｇ
　（8ページ参照）

[作り方]
1　カマスはうろこをとり，背
から開き内臓，エラ，中骨と腹
骨をとる（3枚おろしにして身
だけ使ってもよい）。身の両面
に塩をぬりつけるようにして冷
蔵庫で2，3時間しめる。甘酢
の調味料を合わせてまぜ，砂糖
をとかしておく。
2　1を水洗いして塩を落とし，
水気をふいて甘酢に20分つけ，
小骨をとる。
3　2の身の方にすし飯をつめ，
ラップで巻き1時間くらいおい
てひと口大に切り，盛りつける。
＊好みでカマスの身にワサビを
ぬったり，しそや甘酢しょうが
のせん切りをはさんでもよい。

[Ingredients] 4 servings
2 fresh barracuda
　　(300-400 g/each)
120 g salt
Sugared vinegar
　　200 cc vinegar
　　100 g sugar
　　1 red chilli pepper
700 g *sushi* rice
　　(Refer to p.8)

[Directions]
1　Scale barracudas. Open by cutting along the backbone, clean, and remove small bones and belly bones (or divide the barracuda into three fillets, and use the upper parts, instead of cutting along backbone). Spread salt on both sides of fillets and refrigerate for 2-3 hours. To make sugared vinegar, mix ingredients and dissolve.
2　Wash salt from the fillets, wipe off the moisture, and soak the fillets in sugared vinegar for 20 minutes. Remove small bones.
3　Place *sushi* rice on the inner side of the fillets, roll fillets with plastic wrap, and let stay for 1 hour. Slice into bite-size pieces, and arrange on a plate.
*Variation: *Wasabi* can be spread over the surface of the fillets, or *shiso* or sweet-vinegared ginger slices sand-wiched between the fillets.

くつぞこの煮つけ *Kutsuzoko-no-nitsuke*

Simmered Sole

E 357 kcal ／ DF 1.2 g ／ S 1.9 g （1人分　1 serving）

くつぞこの話　有明海は日本一の干満差と広大な干潟を有し，ムツゴロウ，メカジャ，ウミタケ，ワラスボなど，特有の魚介類がとれる。くつぞこは一般にシタビラメと呼ばれるが，くつ底の形に似ているところから地元では「くつぞこ」と呼ばれる。

Kutsuzoko　Ariakekai (the Sea of Ariake) has vast tidelands and boasts the largest tidal ranges in Japan. Unique seafood, such as *mutsugoro, mekaja, umitake,* and *warasubo,* is caught here. One particular fish, "*shitabirame*", is called "*kutsuzoko*" (literally "sole") in Fukuoka.

[材料] 4人分
くつぞこ（シタビラメ）　4尾
木綿豆腐　½丁
菊菜　120g
調味A　水　150cc
　　　　酒　70cc
　　　　砂糖　30g（大さじ3）
　　　　濃口醤油　45cc（大さじ3）
しょうがのしぼり汁　10cc（小さじ2）

[作り方]
1　くつぞこは包丁でうろこをとり，エ
ラと内臓をとって血のかたまりを水洗い
して水気をふきとり，切り目を入れてお
く。
2　豆腐は4つに切りわけ，菊菜は水洗
いして5cm長さに切る。
3　鍋にAの調味料を入れ強火にかけ，
沸騰したら1を切り目の入った方を上に
して入れる。沸騰してきたらアクをとっ
て落としぶたをし，鍋ぶたをして中火よ
りやや強い火で5分間ぐらい煮る（煮汁
が半量になるぐらい）。
4　3のふたをとり豆腐としょうがのし
ぼり汁を入れ，鍋を傾けて煮汁をすくい，
魚の上から4，5回かける。最後に菊菜
を入れて火を止める。
5　器にくつぞこと豆腐，菊菜を盛り，
上から煮汁をたっぷりかける。

[Ingredients] 4 servings
4 sole
1/2 block *momen* (hard) *tofu*
120 g *shungiku/kikuna* (chrysanthemum leaves)
Seasoning (A)　150 cc water
　　　　　　　70 cc *sake*
　　　　　　　30 g sugar
　　　　　　　45 cc *koikuchi* (strong) soy sauce
10 cc ginger juice

[Directions]
1　Scale the sole with a knife. Clean and wash
well, and remove moisture with a kitchen towel.
Make a cross-shaped incision on one side.
2　Cut *tofu* into 4 pieces. Wash the *kikuna* leaves
in cold water and cut into 5 cm lengths.
3　Mix Seasoning (A) in a pot, bring to a boil, and
add the sole. (The side with an incision should be
on top.) When the liquid comes to a boil, skim off
foam, place a drop-lid on the surface, cover the pan
with another lid, and simmer over mid to high heat
for about 5 minutes or until the liquid is reduced by
about half.
4　Remove the lids and add the *tofu* and ginger
juice. Tilt the pot to skim the simmering liquid, and
ladle about 4-5 scoops of the liquid over the sole.
Then, sprinkle with *kikuna* and turn off the heat.
5　Arrange the sole, *tofu* and *kikuna* on a plate
and pour on the rest of the simmering liquid.

だご汁 *Dago-jiru*
Soup with Dumplings

E 362 kcal ／ DF 6.0 g ／ S 6.4 g （1人分　1 serving）

[材料] 4人分
だいこん　100g
にんじん　50g
白菜　100g
ごぼう　50g
さといも　200g
生しいたけ　4枚
手打ちのだご
　強力粉　150g
　薄力粉　150g
　塩　18g（大さじ1）
　水　130〜140cc
別に打ち粉（強力粉）　少々
いりこだし　1000cc
　（7ページ参照）
田舎味噌　60〜70g
ゆずごしょう
　または七味唐辛子　適量

[作り方]
1　手打ちのだごを作る。ボールにふるった強力粉と薄力粉を入れ，塩をまぜ，水を少しずつ入れながら木杓子でまぜ合わせる。次に手で練り，1つにまとまったら，ラップに包んで30分間おいておく。
2　だいこん，にんじんは4cm長さの短冊に切る。白菜はタテ半分に切り1cm幅に切る。ごぼうは表面の皮をこすりとり，タテ半分に切り，4cm長さのななめ薄切りにし，水につけておく。さといもは皮をむき，塩をふりかけてよくもんで水洗いし，1cm厚さの輪切りにする。生しいたけは石づきをとり，少し厚めの薄切りにする。
3　1を表面がなめらかになり弾力が出るまでよく練る。乾いたまな板の上に打ち粉をし，めん棒で薄くのばし好みの大きさに切っただごをたっぷりの湯でゆでて水にとり，手でもんでぬめりをとりザルにあげる。
4　鍋にいりこだしを入れて2の材料を加え，さといもがやわらかくなるまで煮る。次に味噌をといて味を整え，3のだごを入れ，再び煮立ったら器に盛る。薬味にゆずごしょうや七味唐辛子をそえる。

だご汁の話　昔，農家にとって米は大切な収入源であった。家では米を節約し，裏作として作っていた小麦をだごにして食べた。だご汁は，だいこん，さといもなどの秋の味覚とだごを煮込んだもので，主食兼副食として，寒い時期に何度も食卓に上る料理だった。

Soup with Dumplings

[Ingredients] 4 servings
100 g radishes
50 g carrots
100 g Chinese cabbages
50 g burdock roots
200 g taro potatoes
4 *shiitake* mushrooms
Home-made *dago* dumplings
  150 g hard flour
  150 g soft flour
  18 g salt
  130 -140 cc water
Uchi-ko (hard flour)
1000 cc *iriko dashi* stock
  (Refer to p.7)
60-70 g *inaka miso*
  (*miso* made from barley
  and soy bean)
Yuzu gosho pepper
  or *shichimi* pepper

[Directions]
1　[How to make dago] Sieve soft flour and strong flour together. Pour the flour and salt in a bowl, and add water gradually, mixing with a wooden spatula. Knead the dough thoroughly by hand, forming into a ball. Cover the dough with plastic wrap and let rest for 30 minutes.

2　Cut radishes and carrots into 4 cm length rectangles. Chop Chinese cabbage into half lengthwise, and then cut into 1 cm pieces. Remove the skin of the burdock roots, cut into half lengthwise, slice diagonally into 4 cm length pieces, and soak in water. Peel the taro potatoes, sprinkle with salt, rub in the salt, rinse, and cut into 1 cm thick rings. Cut away any root clusters of *shiitake* mushrooms and slice into pieces.

3　Knead the dough (1) again until the surface is smooth and elastic. Roll out the dough with a rolling pin on a lightly floured dry cutting board and cut into "*dago*" (dumplings) of your desired size. Boil the dumplings in a pot filled with hot water, rinse rub with your hands to remove any slime and then drain in a sieve.

4　Pour *iriko dashi* stock in a pot, add 2, and simmer until the taro potatoes are tender. Dissolve in *miso* to taste, add *dago* (3), and simmer until boiling again. Serve in individual bowls and add *yuzu* pepper or *shichimi* pepper, if desired.

Dago-jiru　In Fukuoka, rice farmers used to grow wheat as an out of season crop for an extra source of income. To conserve rice they boiled autumn seasonal ingredients such as radishes, taro potatoes and *dago* (dumpling cakes made of wheat flour), cooking *dago-jiru* as both a main dish and a side dish. *Dago-jiru* was often served through autumn to winter.

イワシの糠味噌炊き *Iwashi-no-nukamiso-daki*
Sardines Simmered in *Nukamiso* E 272 kcal／DF 1.2 g／S 5.2 g （1人分　1 serving）

[材料] 4人分

マイワシ 250 g	砂糖 40 g
水 150cc	濃口醤油 80cc
酒 150cc	糠味噌 80 g

[作り方]

1　イワシはうろこと頭，内臓をとり，きれいに洗う。

2　鍋に水，酒を入れ，1のイワシを並べ強火にかけ，沸騰してきたら砂糖，醤油を加え中火で5分間煮る。次に糠味噌を加え弱火で20分ぐらい煮る。煮汁が少し残るぐらいで，魚の表面においしそうなつやが出てきたら出来上がり。

＊糠味噌は香りの良いものを使う

[Ingredients] 4 servings

250 g sardines
150 cc water
150 cc *sake*
40 g sugar
80 cc *koikuchi* (strong) soy sauce
80 g *nukamiso*

[Directions]

1　Remove the scales, clean and wash sardines.

2　Arrange sardines (1) in a pot with water and *sake,* and place the pot over high heat. When the liquid comes to a boil, add sugar and soy sauce, and simmer over medium heat for 5 minutes. Add *nukamiso,* and simmer over low heat for 20 minutes. When the liquid thickens into a sauce, the fish is ready.

*Enjoy the fragrant smell of *nukamiso.*

糠味噌炊きの話　北九州市小倉の郷土料理である。この地域では江戸時代から保存食として「糠漬け」が庶民の間に広まっていた。今でも50年，100年と先祖代々受け継がれた香りのよい糠味噌を使って，イワシ，サバなどの糠味噌炊きが作られる。地元では「じんだ煮」とか「おささじ煮」とも呼ばれている。

Iwashi-no-nukamiso-daki　*Nukamiso-daki* is a local specialty of Kokura, Kitakyushu City. Since the Edo era, *Nuka-zuke* (pickles in salted rice-bran paste), has spread among local commoners as a preserved food. Even now, *Nukamiso-daki* is made with sardines or mackerel, using the flavoring of *Nukamiso* which has been handed down by ancestors over the past 50 to 100 years. Local people sometimes call *Nukamiso-daki* "*Jinda-ni*" or "*Osasaji-ni*".

だぶ（らぶ） *Dabu (Rabu)*

Thickened Soup with Vegetables

E 100 kcal ／ DF 3.5 g ／ S 1.3 g （1人分　1 serving）

だぶの話　福岡県内や周辺地域で，特にお祝いのときに同じような料理が作られている。根菜類を1cm角に切り，うす揚げや鶏肉と一緒にいりこだしで煮て，吸い物程度の味付けをする。煮物のような汁物であるが，博多のだぶは葛粉や水溶き片栗粉で少しとろみをつける。だぶだぶした出来上がりなのでこの名があるが，博多では「らぶ」という人もいる。朝倉地方では「くずかけ」，豊前地方では「にぐい」と呼ばれる。くずかけはだぶと同様にとろみをつけるが，にぐいはとろみをつけない。

Dabu　A similar dish is made in Fukuoka prefecture and surrounding areas for special occasions. Root vegetables are cut into 1 cm pieces and boiled in *iriko dashi* stock with deep-fried tofu and chicken and seasoned like *suimono* (clear soup). Hakata's *Dabu* is a soup like *suimono*, but it is thickened with *kuzu* starch or potato starch dissolved in water. It is called "*Dabu*" because of its thick consistency like the Japanese expression *dabudabu*, but in Hakata it is sometimes called "*Rabu*". In the Asakura area it is called "*Kuzukake*" and in the Buzen area, "*Nigui*". *Kuzukake* is thickened like *Dabu*, but *Nigui* is not.

[材料] 4人分
うす揚げ（いなり揚げ）　1枚
にんじん　50g
ごぼう　40g
れんこん　50g
こんにゃく　1/3丁
だいこん　50g
さといも　80g
いりこだし　600cc（7ページ参照）
調味料
　濃口醬油　5〜7cc（小さじ1〜1.5）
　塩　3〜6g（小さじ1/2〜1）
　砂糖　1〜1.5g（小さじ1/3〜1/2）
水溶き片栗粉
　片栗粉　9g（大さじ1）
　だし　30cc（大さじ2）

[作り方]
1　たっぷりのお湯を沸かし，うす揚げを5分間ゆでて油抜きし，1cm角に切る。
2　にんじん，れんこん，こんにゃく，だいこん，さといもは1cm角のさいの目切り，ごぼうは1cm長さに切る。さといもは水からゆで，沸騰したら残りの野菜を加え，1分後にザルにとる。
3　鍋にいりこだしと1，2を加え，さといもが柔らかくなったら調味料を入れて味を調え，水溶き片栗粉でとろみをつける。

[Ingredients]　4 servings
1 deep-fried *tofu* (used for *inarizushi*)
50 g carrots
40 g burdock roots
50 g lotus root
1/3 cake devil's tongue
50 g Japanese radish
80 g taro potatoes
600 cc *iriko dashi* stock　(p.7)
Seasoning
　5-7 cc *koikuchi* (strong) soy sauce
　3-6 g salt
　1-1.5 g sugar
Potato starch dissolved in water
　9 g potato starch
　30 cc *dashi* stock

[Directions]
1　Boil a liberal amount of water, add deep-fried *tofu* and boil for 5 mins. Remove oil from the *tofu* and cut in 1 cm squares.
2　Cut carrots, lotus root, devil's tongue, Japanese radish and taro potatoes into 1 cm squares. Slice burdock roots into 1 cm lengths. Put taro potatoes in water to boil. When the water boils, add the remaining vegetables. Pour through a sieve after one minute.
3　Put *iriko dashi* stock with 1 and 2 into a pot. When the potatoes are tender, add seasonings for flavor and thicken with the potato starch dissolved in water.

博多のおもてなし料理

Traditional Feast of Hakata

吸い物膳の話　福岡（博多）では，かしわご飯に吸い物，がめ煮，ぬたえの一汁二菜の膳を「吸い物膳」として，祭りやお客が来たときのおもてなし料理として出していた。かしわご飯は一般的には鶏の炊き込みご飯といわれるが，海に近い所ではサワラやハイオ（カジキマグロ）を使う。

Suimono zen　In Hakata/Fukuoka, "*Ichiju Nisai*" (one soup and two side-dishes) was served as *Suimonozen* (a set-meal with a clear soup) to celebrate festivals or to make guests welcome. *Suimonozen,* a feast of Hakata, includes *kashiwagohan, osuimono, gameni* and *nutae.* In seaside locations, fish such as *sawara* (Spanish mackerel) and *haio* (spear fish) is used instead of chicken.

吸い物膳

Suimonozen (set menu)

1 かしわご飯
Kashiwagohan
（作り方は52ページ）
(Refer to p.52)

2 お吸い物
Osuimono

3 がめ煮
Gameni
（作り方は72ページ）
(Refer to p.72)

4 ぬたえ
Nutae
（作り方は53ページ）
(Refer to p.53)

お吸い物 *Osuimono*
Clear Soup

E 47 kcal ／ DF 0.1 g ／ S 1.7 g
（1人分　1 serving）

［材料］　4人分
一番だし　600cc
調味A　　塩　3〜4 g（小さじ½〜⅔）
　　　　　酒　5cc（小さじ1）
　　　　　薄口醤油　5cc（小さじ1）
板付かまぼこ（ピンク）　½本
豆腐　⅓丁
春菊　少々

［作り方］
一番だしに調味Aを加え，かまぼこ，豆腐を1cm角に切って入れる。味をみて器に盛り，春菊の葉を2，3枚入れる。

[Ingredients]　4 servings
600 cc *ichiban dashi* (first brew) stock
Seasoning (A)
　3-4 g salt
　5 cc *sake*
　5 cc *usukuchi* (light) soy sauce
1/2 *itatsuki-kamaboko* (fish paste on the plate) *pink colored
1/3 block *tofu*
Shungiku Chrysanthemum leaves

[Directions]
Pour the *ichiban dashi* stock into a pan and add Seasoning (A). Cut *kamaboko* and *tofu* into 1 cm squares and add to the *dashi*. Season to taste, if necessary. Ladle into individual bowls, and sprinkle on a few leaves of *shungiku*.

かしわご飯 *Kashiwa Gohan*
Japanese-style Chicken Rice

E 557 kcal ／ DF 1.5 g ／ S 2.8 g
(1人分　1 serving)

博多のおもてなし料理

Traditional Feast of Hakata

[材料]　4人分
米　3カップ（480 g）
鶏モモ肉　200 g
にんじん　60 g
たけのこ　80 g（またはごぼう50 g）
A　だし　100cc
　　酒　15cc（大さじ1）
　　濃口醤油　45cc（大さじ3）
　　砂糖　9 g（大さじ1）
B　作り方3の残り煮汁＋だし
　　合計3.6カップ（米の1.2倍）
　　塩　6 g（小さじ1）

[作り方]
1　米は炊く1時間前に洗い，水気を
切っておく。
2　鶏肉は2cm幅の薄切り，にんじん，
たけのこは2cm長さの細切りにする
（ごぼうを使う場合は，小さくささ
がきにして水にさらす。固いときはさっ
とゆでる）。
3　鍋にAを入れて火にかけ，鶏肉，
にんじん，たけのこの順に入れる。具
が煮えたらアミでこし，具と汁に分け
る。
4　炊飯器にBと米を入れてよくまぜ
る。
5　4の上に具を加えて炊き，10分間
蒸らす。好みでもみのりやねぎの小口
切りを散らす。

[Ingredients]　4 servings
480 g rice
200 g chicken thighs
60g carrots
80 g bamboo shoots
　(or 50 g burdock roots)
Seasoning (A)
　100 cc *dashi* stock
　15 cc *sake*
　45 cc *koikuchi* (strong) soy sauce
　9 g sugar
Seasoning (B)
　Liquid for cooking rice (water + left
　over soup stock of Seasoning A)
　720 cc (3.6 cup) *1.2 times of rice
6 g salt

[Directions]
1　Wash the rice 60 minutes prior to
cooking and drain with a sieve.
2　Chop chicken into 2 cm widths.
Thinly slice carrots and bamboo
shoots into 2 cm lengths. (In case of
using burdock instead of bamboo
shoots, shave and soak in water to
get rid of any bitterness. When too
hard, parboil.)
3　Pour Seasoning (A) into a pot,
add chicken, carrots and bamboo
shoots in that order, and simmer.
Turn off the heat, divide the solids
and liquids with a sieve, and prepare
Seasoning (B).
4　Pour Seasoning (B) and rice into
the rice cooker and mix well.
5　Place toppings (the solids in 3)
on 4, cook the rice, and allow the
cooked rice to settle for 10 minutes.
Top with *mominori* seaweeds and/or
thinly sliced green onions if desired.

52

ぬたえ *Nutae*

Sweet and Sour *Miso* Salad

E 96 kcal ／ DF 1.6 g ／ S 4.9 g
（1 人分　1 serving）

[材料] 4 人分
イワシ（20cmぐらい）　1 尾
　（またはイカ，コノシロ）
塩　18 g（大さじ 1）
酢　15cc（大さじ 1）
だいこん　220 g
にんじん　30 g
小ねぎ　2 本
炒りごま　10 g（大さじ 1½）
調味A　白味噌　30 g（大さじ 1½）
　　　　酢　30cc（大さじ 2）
　　　　砂糖　20 g（大さじ 2）
　　　　水　15cc（大さじ 1）

[作り方]
1　イワシは手開きにし，たっぷりの塩を両面にぬり15分おいておく。次に塩を水で洗い落とし，酢を15ccかけて 5 分おき，細切りにする。
2　だいこん，にんじんは 4 cm長さ，3 ㎜幅の短冊に切り，塩もみして水洗いし，水気をよく切っておく。
3　炒りごまをすり鉢ですり，調味Aを入れてよくすりまぜる。1 と 2 を加えて和え器に盛り，小ねぎの小口切りを上にふる。
＊イカのときは細切りにしてさっとゆがいて使う。

[Ingredients]　4 servings
1 sardine (20 cms) (or squid, *konoshiro* or mango fish)
18 g salt
15 cc vinegar
220 g Japanese radishes
30 g carrots
2 *konegi* leeks
10 g roasted sesame
Seasoning (A)　30 g white *miso*
　　　　　　　　30 cc vinegar
　　　　　　　　20 g sugar
　　　　　　　　15 cc water

[Directions]
1　Split sardines into two pieces lengthwise with your hands, spread plenty of salt over the surface of both sides, and leave for 15 minutes. Wash the salt off, sprinkle vinegar (15 cc) on the surface, let stand for 5 minutes, and then slice the fish meat thinly.
2　Chop Japanese radishes and carrots 4 cm long and 3 mm thick, rub with salt, rinse and drain.
3　Grind the parched sesame in a grinding bowl with a pestle, add Seasoning (A), and mix well to make the sesame sauce. Dress 1 and 2 with the sesame sauce, and sprinkle with sliced *konegi* leek.
*When using squid instead of sardines, slice thinly and parboil.

ぬたえの話　ぬたえは「ぬた和え」，または短くして「ぬた」とも呼ばれ，ぬたは漢字で「沼田」と書く。福岡（博多）の正月や祝いのときに作られる。また，「お酢和え」は，精進のときに出される和え物で，魚の代わりに薄揚げを使い，ごま酢で味つけをする。

Nutae　*Nutae,* also called *Nuta-ae* or *Nuta,* is cooked for the New Year holidays and for ceremonies in Fukuoka/Hakata. A variation is *Osuae,* which is served with Buddhist vegetarian dishes with *usuage* (thin-sliced fried *tofu*) instead of fish meat, and dressed in a sour sesame sauce.

博多の名物

博多で「ごりょんさん」といえば，商家の奥さんのこと。ごりょんさんは食べ物を無駄にしないでおいしい料理を作る。その代表的なものの1つに「がめ煮（筑前煮）」がある。博多では，正月や祭りに作られる祝い事の料理である。

博多の鍋物で有名なのは水炊き。博多では，店でも家庭でも味わえる。

そして，博多の一番の名物といえば博多ラーメン。その特徴は豚骨スープと細麺にある。博多の屋台で注文するときは，「ヤワ」「カタ」「バリカタ」など，麺のゆで加減を指定する。また，替え玉といって，スープを残して麺だけを追加注文する。

関東のうどんに比べて，博多のうどんは麺がやわらかい。すめ（だし汁のこと）はサバ節，カツオ節，アゴ（トビウオ），昆布などでとり，薄味だが良い香りがある。博多うどんの代表的な具はごぼう天（ごぼうの天ぷら）と丸天（魚のすり身を丸くして揚げたもの）である。

Specialties of Hakata

The term "*goryonsan*" refers to the wives of prosperous merchant families in the Hakata district. *Goryonsan* cook delicious dishes without wasting ingredients. "*Gameni*" or "*chikuzen-ni*" is one of their local specialties. In Hakata, *gameni* is a festive dish cooked for the New Year holidays and other special occasions.   Another famous dish is *Mizutaki,* a type of "*nabemono*" or winter cuisine served in a large pot. We can have *Mizutaki* at local restaurants as well as at home.

The best-known specialty in Hakata is perhaps *Hakata ramen* noodles. It features a pork bone broth (*tonkotsu* soup) and thin noodles. When you order *Hakata ramen* at *Yatai* food stalls in Hakata, you need to specify how you want the noodles boiled, "*yawa*" (soft), "*kata*" (hard) or "*bari-kata*" (very hard). The term "*kaedama*" is used when you want a refill of noodles added to your remaining broth.

Compared to *Udon* noodles in the Kanto region, *Hakata udon* noodles are soft. "*Sume*", which refers to the broth, is made from dried mackerel, dried bonito, dried flying fish, and dried kelp and has a light taste but good aroma. Typical toppings of *Hakata udon* are "*gobo-ten*", or burdock root *tempura*, and "*maru-ten*", or fried fish paste.

冬
Winter

雪の光明禅寺
Snow-covered *Komyozenji* Temple

もつ鍋 *Motsunabe*　　E 653 kcal ／ DF 5.9 g ／ S 4.7 g （1 人分　1 serving）
Beef Offal Hot Pot

もつ鍋の話　ルーツは，うどんを入れて煮込む「テッチャンチゲ」という朝鮮の家庭料理や，炭鉱労働者が当時は捨てられていた牛・豚の内臓（放〔ほお〕るもん）で作っていた「トンちゃん」などといわれる。野菜たっぷりでカロリーも低く，ヘルシーということで若い女性に人気となり全国に広まった。

Motsunabe　There are several different stories as to the origins of *motsunabe*. Some say it comes from a Korean home-made dish called "Doenjang jjigae" made with udon noodles. Others credit its origins to "Tonchan", which was cooked by mineworkers with discarded ("*houru*" or dumped) beef and pork offal. As *Motsunabe* is a healthy low-calorie pot dish full of vegetables, it has become popular among young ladies, and can now be enjoyed anywhere in Japan.

[材料]　4人分
牛もつ（下ゆでしてあるもの）　500ｇ
　　牛のシマ腸（大腸），丸腸（小腸），
　　センマイ（胃），レバー，ハツ（心臓）
キャベツ　1/2個
にら　2束
もやし　150ｇ
白ねぎ　1本
絹ごし豆腐　1丁
にんにく　2片
赤唐辛子　3，4本
だし　1000cc
調味Ａ
　　酒　100cc
　　濃口醬油　100cc
　　みりん　50cc
　　白味噌　10ｇ（大さじ1/2）
　　塩　3ｇ（小さじ1/2）
　　こしょう　少々
チャンポン玉　3玉

[作り方]
1　牛もつはさっとゆでてザルにとる。
2　キャベツは6㎝長さ，3㎝幅に切
る。にらは6㎝長さ，白ねぎはななめ
切り，豆腐はひと口大に切る。にんに
くは薄切りにしておく。
3　鍋にだしと調味Ａを入れ，1，2と
赤唐辛子をのせ強火にかける。沸騰し
てきたらアクをとり，中火にする。た
っぷりの野菜が沈み，やわらかくなっ
てきたら汁とともに器にとり食べる。
4　最後はチャンポンを煮て食べる。
＊もつ鍋は醬油，味噌味，スキ焼き
風といろいろな食べ方がある。スープ
は市販品を使ってもよい。

[Ingredients]　4 servings
500 g beef internal organs
　　large intestines, small intestines, stomach,
　　liver, and heart (parboiled)
1/2 head cabbage
2 bunches *nira* (Chinese chive)
150 g bean sprouts
1 *shironegi* leek
1 block *kinugoshi* (soft) *tofu*
2 cloves garlic
3-4 red chilli peppers
1000 cc *dashi* stock
Seasoning (A)
　　100 cc *sake*
　　100 cc *koikuchi* (strong) soy sauce
　　50 cc *mirin* (sweet cooking sake)
　　10 g *shiro* (white) *miso*
　　3 g salt
　　Pepper
3 packages *champon* (Chinese noodles)

[Directions]
1　Parboil beef internal organs and drain with a sieve.
2　Chop cabbage into pieces 6 cm in length and 3 cm in width. Slice Chinese chives into 6 cm pieces. Slice *shironegi* leeks diagonally. Cut *tofu* into bite-sized pieces. Slice the garlic thinly.
3　Pour *dashi* stock and Seasoning (A) into a pot, add the ingredients 1 and 2, and simmer over high heat. When the liquid boils, skim off any foam, and turn down the heat to medium. Serve the soup with the other ingredients in individual bowls when the vegetables are tender and sink down to the bottom of the pot.
4　When all the ingredients are eaten up, add *champon* noodles, and serve.
*Variation: *Motsunabe* dishes can be made with various kinds of seasoning, including soy-sauce, *miso*, and *sukiyaki* stock. *Dashi* stocks for *motsunabe* available in the market can be used instead of home-made *dashi* stock.

鶏ちり *Torichiri*　　　E 600 kcal ／ DF 8.2 g ／ S 5.9 g　（1人分　1 serving）
Chicken Hot Pot

[材料] 4人分
地鶏モモ肉　400g
鶏がら　400g
白菜　400g
たまねぎ　1玉（200g）
糸こんにゃく　1袋
もやし（細め）　1袋
青ねぎ　5本
焼き豆腐　½丁
水　1500cc
砂糖　75g
濃口醤油　100cc
そうめん　200g

[Ingredients] 4 servings
400 g chicken legs
400 g chicken bones
400 g Chinese cabbage
200 g onions
1 package *konnyaku* noodles
1 package bean sprouts (thin)
5 green onions
1 block *yaki-tofu*
1500 cc water
75 g sugar
100 cc *koikuchi* (strong) soy sauce
200 g *somen* (fine wheat) noodles

[作り方]
1　地鶏肉は食べやすい大きさにそぎ切りにする。白菜はタテ半分に切り4〜5cmの長さに，たまねぎはくし形に，青ねぎは4〜5cmの長さに切る。糸こんにゃくは5分間ゆでてザルにとる。そうめんは固めにゆでておく。
2　鍋に1500ccの水，地鶏，がらを入れ，1時間，アクをとりながらやわらかくなるまで煮てスープを作る。
3　2から鶏がらをとり出し，スープ1200ccに砂糖，醤油を入れて5分間煮る。糸こんにゃく，たまねぎ，白菜，もやし，豆腐の順に加え，最後に青ねぎを入れる。そうめんは食べる分だけ入れ，さっと煮て食べる。途中で地鶏肉を追加してもよい。

[Directions]
1　Slice chicken diagonally into strips. Chop a head of Chinese cabbage into halves, and cut into 4-5 cm slices. Cut onions into wedges. Slice green onions into 4-5 cm lengths. Boil *konnyaku* noodles for 5 minutes, and drain with a sieve. Half-boil the *somen* noodles.
2　Pour 1500 cc water into an earthen pot, add chicken legs and bones, and simmer for 1 hour, skimming off foam until the meat is tender.
3　Remove the chicken bone from 2. Add sugar and soy sauce to 1200 cc of the stock and boil for 5 minutes. Add the *konnyaku* noodles, onions, Chinese cabbage, bean sprouts, and *tofu* in that order, and finally, add green onions. When serving *somen,* ladle bite-size pieces, dip quickly in the boiling soup, and eat. Add chicken, if desired.

鶏ちりの話　福岡（博多）は古くから遣唐使や朝鮮通信使など大陸との渡来が盛んで，海外使節や貿易などを通じて海外の食文化が入ってきた。インド原産といわれるニワトリも，古くから福岡で飼育され，そのため鶏料理が多く見られる。鶏ちりは少し甘めのスキ焼き風の味つけで，似たような鶏鍋が農山村に多く残っている。

Torichiri　Fukuoka/Hakata has a long history of mutual visits to and from the Asian continent, including a Japanese envoy to China in the Tang Dynasty and an envoy to Korea in the Joseon Dynasty, and foreign food culture has been imported through these envoys and by trading. Chicken, which is said to have originated in India, has been bred in the Fukuoka area for a long time, so we can enjoy chicken dishes here as a local specialty. *Torichiri* has a rather sweet taste like *Sukiyaki.* Many *torichiri*-like hot pot dishes still remain in farm and mountain villages.

水炊き *Mizutaki*

E 516 kcal ／ DF 5.2 g ／ S 0.5 g （1人分　1 serving）

Chicken-broth Hot Pot

[材料] 4人分
若鶏骨つき肉　1kg
スープ
　鶏がら　600g
　水　2000cc
　塩　ひとつまみ
砂ずり，肝　2羽分
豆腐　1丁
春菊　1/2束
生しいたけ　4枚
白菜　1/4株
カリフラワー　150g
ポン酢醤油　適量
小ねぎ(小口切り)　20g
紅葉おろし
　だいこん　100g
　赤唐辛子　2本
(好みで)小もち　4個

[作り方]
1　鶏がらを熱湯で洗い，水を入れて強火で炊きアクをとり，3分の1の量になるまで煮つめてスープを作る。途中でがらをすりこぎで砕き，スープの中に入れ，白くなるまで煮込んでこす。
2　鶏肉は1個50gぐらいにぶつ切りにし，深鍋に入れて2倍くらいの湯を入れ，アクをとりながら強火で25分くらい煮る。火を止めた後30分くらいつけておくと骨離れがよくなる。
3　砂ずり，肝はそぎ切りにして血抜きをし，ゆでて器に盛る。
4　野菜や豆腐は大きめに切り器に盛り，紅葉おろしと小ねぎをそえて出す。
5　食卓用の鍋に2を移し，1のスープを加えて煮ながらポン酢醤油をつけて食べる。途中から豆腐や野菜も加えて煮ながら食べる。
＊鍋の後はもち，うどんなどを入れたり，雑炊にしたりするとおいしい。

水炊きの話　水炊きは全国的にも有名な福岡の郷土料理で，ルーツは中国風の鶏の煮物とか洋風のコンソメスープとかいわれる。澄んだスープをベースにするものと，白濁したスープをベースにするものとがある。最初においしいスープを楽しむのが本来の食べ方。次に鶏肉を食べ，スープの味が濃くなったところで野菜を煮て食べる。鍋の後は雑炊にしたり，うどんを入れたりして食べる。

Chicken-broth Hot Pot

[Ingredients] 4 servings
1 kg chicken with bones
Soup stock
　600 g chicken bone
　2000 cc water
　Pinch salt
50 g chicken liver
50 g chicken gizzards
1 block *tofu*
1/2 bunch *shungiku/kikuna*
　(chrysanthemum) leaves
4 *shiitake* mushrooms
1/4 head of Chinese cabbage
150 g cauliflower
Ponzu soy sauce
　(sauce containing soy sauce
　and vinegar or citrus juice)
20 g sliced *konegi* leek
Momiji oroshi
　100 g grated radish
　2 red peppers
(4 rice cakes)

[Directions]
1　Rinse chicken bones in hot water in a pot. Add the cold water to the pot and boil over high heat, skim off any foam, and simmer until the liquid is reduced to 1/3. While simmering, take chicken bones out of the pot, grind with a pestle, and put back into the pot. When the soup turns milky, strain.
2　Chop chicken into pieces (about 50 g), and place in a deep pot. Add hot water to twice the depth of the chicken and simmer over high heat while skimming off any foam for 25 minutes. Turn off the heat and leave for 30 minutes, so that the bone can be removed from the chicken easily.
3　Shave chicken liver and gizzards thinly with a knife, let bleed, boil, and then drain.
4　Chop vegetables and *tofu* into chunks, arrange on a plate, and serve with *momiji oroshi* and sliced *konegi* leek.
5　Put 2 into the earthen pot, and add stock (1) and the meat (3). While simmering, enjoy ingredients in *ponzu* soy sauce. Add *tofu* and vegetables to the pot, and enjoy the dish while it simmers over low heat in the middle of the dining table.
*After finishing the ingredients, *mochi* rice cakes or *udon* noodles can be added. Rice porridge can also be made with the stock.

Mizutaki　*Mizutaki* is a nationally-known Fukuoka cuisine. The origin is said to be Chinese-style cooked chicken or a Western style of consomme soup. *Mizutaki* can be made with two kinds of stock: a clear soup or milky chicken broth soup. To enjoy *Mizutaki,* taste the soup before eating the chicken, and when the taste of the soup has become strong enough, add vegetables to the soup. After enjoying all these ingredients, use the soup for *Zousui* (rice porridge) or *udon* noodles.

七草汁
Nanakusa jiru

Nanakusa Soup

E 42 kcal ／ DF 2.6 g ／ S 1.9 g
（1 人分　1 serving）

［材料］ 4 人分
春の七草　200 g
　せり
　なずな（ぺんぺん草）
　ごぎょう（ははこ草）
　はこべら（はこべ）
　ほとけのざ
　すずな（かぶの葉）
　すずしろ（だいこんの葉）
いりこだし　600cc
　（7 ページ参照）
合わせ味噌　50〜60 g

［作り方］
1　春の七草はさっとゆでて
水にとり水気をしぼり，小口
切りにする。
2　いりこだしをとって 1 の
七草を加え，味噌をといて仕
上げる。
＊七草がゆにするときは，白
がゆを作り，塩と薄口醬油で
味をつけ，七草を加える。

[Ingredients] 4 servings
200 g *nanakusa* (seven spring herbs)
　Seri, nazuna, gogyo, hakobe, hotokenoza,
　suzuna, suzushiro
600 cc *iriko dashi* stock
　(Refer to p.7)
50-60 g *awase* (mixed) *miso*

[Directions]
1　Parboil *nanakusa,* rinse, drain, and
chop into pieces.
2　Make *iriko dashi* stock, and dissolve
miso into the stock.
*Variation: To make *nanakusa* porridge,
cook rice porridge with salt and light soy
sauce to taste, and add *nanakusa* herbs.

七草汁の話　1 月 7 日の朝，家族の健康や幸せを願って七草汁，または七草がゆを食
べる。歴史的には平安時代の宮中儀式に見られ，江戸時代には広く庶民の間でも食べ
られるようになった。寒い時期に芽を出す若葉の生命力が邪気を払うといわれている。

Nanakusa soup　In Japan, there is a custom of eating *Nanakusajiru* or *Nana-*
kusagayu (soup or rice porridge with seven herbs), in the morning on January
7th to wish health and happiness for family members. Historically, the custom
became established at ceremonies at the Imperial Palace during the Heian
period, and then became widely accepted by ordinary people in the Edo era.
It is believed that young leaves coming out in the cold weather expel evil
spirits.

ごぼう天うどん *Gobo-ten Udon*
Burdock Root *Tempura Udon*

E 378 kcal ／ DF 4.2 g ／ S 3.6 g （1人分　1 serving）

写真手前がごぼう天うどん，奥は丸天うどん
Pictured in the frot is *gobo-ten udon*. In the back is *maruten udon*.

[材料] 4人分
うどん(ゆでたもの)　4玉(1玉約150g)
つゆ　(出来上がり1000cc)
　昆布　12g
　いりこ　20g
　カツオ節(削り)　12g
　サバ節(削り)　8g
　水　1200cc
　＊あご(トビウオを焼いて干したもの)が
　　あれば内臓をとって4〜5つくらいに
　　ちぎり,いりこと一緒に使うと風味が
　　増す。
調味
　みりん　30cc
　薄口醤油　50cc
　塩　2〜3g
　好みで砂糖　5〜10g
ごぼうの天ぷら
　ごぼう　100g
　塩　ひとつまみ
　天ぷら粉(市販品)　100g
　別に小麦粉か天ぷら粉(下衣用)　30g
　揚げ油　500cc
青ねぎ(小口切り)　4本分

[作り方]
▷つゆ
1　いりこは頭と内臓をとり，水，昆布と
ともに鍋に入れて強火にかける。
2　沸騰直前に昆布をとり出し，中火でアク
をすくいながら5分間煮る。次にカツオ
節とサバ節を入れ，中火のまま20秒間煮て
味を出し，ペーパータオルでこす。
3　鍋にみりんを入れて強火にかけ，沸騰
してきたら2のだしを加え，薄口醤油と
塩を入れる(うどんつゆの味は少し飲んで
みて，お吸い物より少し塩味を濃いめに仕
上げる。甘めが好きな人は砂糖を加える)。
▷ごぼうの天ぷら
1　ごぼうは外側をたわしなどでよく洗う
(皮の部分に香りがあるので皮はむかない)。
8cm長さ3mm厚さのななめ切りにして水に
つける。
2　天ぷらの衣は水をやや少なめにして固
めに仕上げる。
3　1のごぼうの水気をふき，軽く塩を
して下衣の小麦粉をつけ，2の衣をつけて
170℃の油で20秒間揚げる。
▷仕上げ
たっぷりのお湯を沸かし，うどんの玉を温
め，器に入れて熱々のつゆを加え，ごぼう
天をのせて青ねぎの小口切りを飾る。好み
で七味唐辛子，一味唐辛子，ゆずごしょう
などを使うとよい。

博多のうどんの話　博多のうどんは麺がやわらかく，すめ(うどんつゆのこと)は，色は
薄いがうまみと香りがある。福岡は小麦の栽培が盛んで，小麦粉を使った料理やおやつが多
くある。博多の名刹・承天寺(福岡市博多区)の開山として知られる鎌倉時代の僧・聖一国
師(円爾弁円)は，中国からうどん・そばの作り方を持ち帰り，広めたとされる。承天寺境
内には今も「饂飩蕎麦発祥之地碑」が立つ。また，博多のうどんのトッピングとして特徴的
なものにごぼう天や丸天がある。丸天は魚のすり身を使った丸い形の天ぷらである。博多で
は魚の練り物を揚げたものを「天ぷら」と呼ぶ。

Burdock Root *Tempura Udon*

[Ingredients] 4 servings

4 packages boiled *udon* noodles
 (150 g/package)
Tsuyu (1000 cc)
 12 g *konbu* kelp
 12 g dried bonito flakes
 20g *iriko* dried sardine
 8 g dried mackerel flakes
 1200 cc water
 *Cooking Hint: If *ago* (flying fish which has
 been grilled and dried) is available, remove
 the entrails, break into 4-5 pieces and use
 along with *iriko* for even more flavor.
Seasoning
 30 cc *mirin* (sweet cooking sake)
 50 cc *usukuchi* (light) soy sauce
 2-3 g salt
 5-10 g sugar (to taste)
Gobo (burdock root) *tempura*
 100 g burdock roots
 Pinch salt
 100 g *tempura* flour *commercially available
 30 g wheat flour or tempura flour
 (for the batter)
 500 cc cooking oil
4 green scallions (cut into small rounds)

[Directions]
▷*Tsuyu*
1 Pinch away or remove the head and entrails from the *iriko* and put in a pot with water and kelp over high heat.
2 Take out the kelp just before boiling and remove the foam while simmering another 5 mins over medium heat. Add dried bonito and dried mackerel and simmer over medium heat for 20 mins to bring out flavor. Strain through a paper towel.
3 Put *mirin* in a pot over high heat. When it comes to a boil, add 2, light soy sauce and salt. (The *udon tsuyu* should taste slightly saltier than *osuimono*. For those who like a sweeter taste, add sugar.)
▷ *Gobo Tempura*
1 Scrub the skin of the burdock root (Do not peel as the skin is flavorful). Cut diagonally in 8-cm by 3-mm pieces and soak in water.
2 Mix *tempura* flour with a small amount of water.
3 Dry the burdock roots from 1, salt lightly, cover with flour, and then dip in 2 and fry at 170℃ for 20 seconds.
To finish, boil a liberal amount of water and heat the *udon* noodles. Put the udon in bowls, pour on piping hot *tsuyu*, pile on the *gobo-ten* and garnish with green scallions. *Ichimi* pepper, *shichimi* pepper, or *yuzu gosho* can be added for flavor.

Hakata Udon   *Hakata udon* noodles are soft and the *sume* (*udon tsuyu* or broth) is mild, yet flavorful and fragrant. In Fukuoka the production of flour is thriving, so there are an abundance of dishes and sweets using flour. It is said that the recipe for *udon* was brought back from China by Shoichi Kokushi (Enni Ben'en), a Buddhist priest of the Kamakura Era and founder of one of Hakata's famous temples, Jotenji Temple (Hakata Ward, Hakata). Even now we can see a stone monument commemorating the birth of *udon* and *soba* on Jotenji's temple grounds. *Hakata udon* is known for having *gobo-ten* or *maruten* as a topping. *Maruten* is a kind of *tempura* made with ground fish paste. In Hakata, fried fish paste is referred to as *tempura*.

せんぶきまげ *Senbukimage*

Green Onions in a *Miso* Sauce

E 157 kcal／DF 2.2 g／S 7.8 g （1人分　1 serving）

[材料]　4人分
わけぎ　20本（約160 g）
アサリ　1 kg
辛子酢味噌　白味噌　80 g
　　　　　　砂糖　20 g（大さじ2）
　　　　　　練り辛子　5 g（大さじ1/2）
　　　　　　酢　45〜60cc（大さじ3〜4）

[作り方]
1　わけぎは色よく塩ゆでし，ザルにあげ風をあて冷ます。わけぎの先端を少し切り，根元から先に向かって包丁の背でしごき，中のぬめりをとる。
2　1の根元を3つに折り，残った部分をぐるぐる巻きつける。
3　アサリはゆでて口が開いたらザルにあげ，身をとり出す。
4　辛子酢味噌を作る。すり鉢に白味噌，砂糖，練り辛子を入れてよくすり，少しずつ酢を加えのばしていく。
5　器にアサリとわけぎを盛り，辛子酢味噌をそえる。

せんぶきまげの話　わけぎのことを福岡では「せんぶき」と呼ぶ。ねぎの変種で，ねぎよりやわらかく甘味がある。2〜3月がおいしくなり，このせんぶきを曲げて盛りつけるため「せんぶきまげ」という料理名がついた。昔はタニシ（水田や沼などにいる淡水の巻き貝）をゆがいて一緒に食べていたが，今はもだま（サメの身のぶつ切りをゆがいたもの），アサリのむき身などを使う。

[Ingredients]　4 servings
20 green onions (*wakegi*)
150 g *shucked* littleneck
Karashi-sumiso dressing
　　80 g *shiro* (white) *miso* paste
　　20 g sugar
　　5 g Japanese kneaded mustard
　　45 cc - 60 cc vinegar

[Directions]
1　Parboil green onions in lightly salted water, drain with a sieve, and leave to cool. Insert the tip of a knife into one end of the green onions, and move the blunt edge slightly to remove the slack (sticky part) of the onions.
2　Fold the green parts of the onions up twice to form 3 parts, and twist the rest of the onion around the folded parts.
3　Parboil shucked littlenecks, rinse, and drain with a sieve.
4　[How to make *karashi-sumiso* dressing] Pour *shiro miso*, sugar and kneaded mustard into a grinding bowl (a mortar), and grind well. Add vinegar gradually until the mixture is smooth.
5　Arrange littlenecks and green onion with *karashi-sumiso* dressing.

Senbukimage　*Wakegi* (green onion) is called "*senbuki*" in Fukuoka. A variety of leek but softer and slightly sweeter than other leek varieties, *senbuki* is in season from February to March. "*Senbuki-mage*" (curl) is a dish with curled *senbuki,* hence its name. Once boiled *tanishi* (river snails found in rice paddies and ponds) were added to *Senbuki-mage*; now *modama* (chopped and boiled shark meat), or *asari* (shucked littlenecks) are used instead of *tanishi.*

正月料理

New Year's Treat

■ おせち　*Osechi*

■ 抹茶富士羹　*Maccha Hujikan*
〔作り方は69ページ〕　(Refer to p.69)

■ 博多雑煮　*Hakata Zoni*
〔作り方は70ページ〕　(Refer to p.70)

■ がめ煮　*Game-ni*
〔作り方は72ページ〕　(Refer to p.72)

おせち料理の話　おせち（御節）とはもともと中国から伝わった節句のことで，季節の変わり目を祝う行事である。現在はそのうちの正月の料理が「おせち料理」と呼ばれている。数の子（子孫繁栄）や黒豆（マメに働けるように），エビ（長寿の象徴），紅白かまぼこなど，縁起が良い食べ物を重箱に入れて出す。また，正月に火を使わなくてすむよう，それぞれが日持ちするように工夫されている。

Osechi　*Osechi*, which originates from ancient China, is a seasonal festival celebrating the turning of the year. Currently, we call the festive foods "*Osechi Ryori*". Lucky ingredients are placed in a *jubako* box: *kazunoko* (herring roe as a symbol of family prosperity), *kuromame* (*mame* meaning not only "bean" but also dedication), *ebi* (shrimp as a symbol of longevity), and red and white *kamaboko* fish paste (the combination of red & white are lucky colors for the Japanese). All dishes are prepared in a manner to keep well, as wisdom from ancient times dictates that the Japanese not cook during the New Year holidays.

抹茶富士羹 *Maccha Fujikan*   E 270 kcal ／ DF 1.0 g ／ S 0.1 g （1 人分　1 serving）

Maccha Fuji Jelly and Meringue

[材料]　4 人分
寒天　1 本　　砂糖　10 g
水　400cc　　抹茶　10 g
砂糖　240 g　牛乳　100cc
卵白　1/2個　富士の型　1 個

[Ingredients] 4 servings
1 stick agar
400 cc water
240 g sugar
1/2 egg white
10 g sugar
10 g Maccha tea powder
100 cc milk
1 *Fuji-san* (mountain-shaped) mold

[作り方]
1　寒天は水（分量外）につけて戻しておく（1 時間）。
2　鍋に水400ccを入れ，1の寒天の水分をよく切ってちぎり入れ，中火でとかす。寒天がとけてから砂糖240 gを加え，砂糖がとけたらこして鍋に戻し，中火のまま3分間煮つめる。
3　卵白をボールに入れて泡立てる。よく泡が立ったら砂糖10 gを加えさらにまぜ，メレンゲ状態にする。2の寒天液100ccをゆっくり入れる。泡立て器で混ぜ，少しとろみがついたら手早く富士の型に流し入れて固め，泡雪羹を作る。
4　抹茶を小さな器に入れ，少し温めた牛乳で「だま」がないようにとき，2の寒天液の残りと合わせる。
5　3に4の寒天液の3分の1ぐらいを流し入れる。少し間をおいて表面の湯気が出なくなったら，残りの寒天液を2回に分けて同じ要領で流し入れる。
6　全体がよく固まったら型から出し，好みの大きさに切る。

＊この料理と富士の型は、中村学園の創立者・中村ハル考案のものである。

[Directions]
1　Reconstitute the agar in a separate amount of water.
2　Put 400 cc water in a pot. Pat the agar dry, break into pieces and dissolve in water over medium heat. Add 240 g sugar and when dissolved, pour through a sieve. Return to heat and simmer over medium heat for 3 minutes.
3　Whisk the egg in a bowl. When many bubbles form, add 10 g sugar and mix until it forms a meringue. Gradually add 100 cc agar liquid 2. Mix with a whisk and when the mixture thickens slightly, quickly pour into the mountain-shaped mold.
4　Put maccha into a small bowl and mix well in warmed milk. Add to the remaining agar liquid 2, making sure there are no lumps.
5　Pour 1/3 agar liquid 4 onto the hardened mixture 3 (*awayuki*) in the mold. When the surface vapor has evaporated, repeat the process twice.
6　When the mixture is set, remove from the mold and cut in individual servings.

*This recipe and *Fuji-san* mountain mold are the brainchild of Haru Nakamura, the founder of Nakamura Gakuen.

正月料理

New Year's Treat

博多雑煮 *Hakata Zoni*
Hakata-style Rice Cake Soup

E 223 kcal ／ DF 1.6 g ／ S 2.2 g （1人分　1 serving）

博多雑煮の話　日本のお正月に食べられるお雑煮は，各地方，各家庭によってさまざまな作り方がある。いわば，その家の歴史がお雑煮にこめられている。博多の雑煮は五目雑煮ともいわれ，多くの食材が使われている。これは博多商人のきっぷのよさ，豪快さを表す，手間と材料を惜しまない雑煮である。特徴をいくつかあげると，まず，だしは「アゴだし」。焼いたトビウオを干したものと昆布，カツオ節でとる。具は「塩ブリ」。ブリは大きくなるにしたがって魚の名前が変わる出世魚である。その他，タイ，アラを使うところもある。緑野菜として使うのはこの地方独特の「カツオ菜（勝男菜）」。もちは家庭円満にということで，「丸もち」をゆでて使う。

Hakata zoni　*Ozoni/zoni*, soup with *mochi* rice cake and vegetables eaten on New Year's holidays, has different tastes from region to region and from family to family. In a way, you can say that *ozoni* showcases your family history. *Hakata zoni* is also called "Assorted *Zoni*", as you can put in various ingredients. Cooking *Hakata zoni* with its rich ingredients needs time and effort, so it shows the generous and big-hearted nature of Hakata merchants. Soup is generally made using the soup of *ago* (dried frying fish)-*dashi*, dried *konbu* kelp, and dried bonito. Ingredients include salted *buri* (adult yellow-tail), which is a symbol of social success because it is called different names at different stages of its growth. Some areas use *tai* (sea-beam) or *ara* (deep-sea bass), instead of *buri*. The Fukuoka indigenous vegetable, "*katsuona*" is added as a green vegetable. In this dish, round-shaped *mochi* rice cakes are used after boiling. The shape of the rice cakes symbolizes "household harmony".

70

[材料] 4人分
丸もち(小)　4個
塩ブリ　120g
さといも(1個50gぐらい)　2個
にんじん　40g
干ししいたけ　4枚
カツオ菜　150g
板付かまぼこ　1/2本
アゴだし　水　1200cc
　　　　　カツオ節　7g
　　　　　焼きアゴ　3匹
　　　　　昆布　10g(10cm角1枚)
調味A　塩　5g(小さじ2/3〜1)
　　　　酒　8cc(小さじ1 1/2)
　　　　濃口醤油　8cc(小さじ1 1/2)
ゆず　1/4個
竹串　4本

[作り方]
1　だし汁を作る。鍋に水を用意し,昆布を入れ,焼きアゴは,腸をとりのぞいて小さくさき,昆布とともに水につけておく。このまま火にかけ,沸騰直前に昆布をとり出し,5〜6分弱火で煮出し,カツオ節を加え1分くらい煮て火を止め,5分程度おいておく。これを静かにこし,雑煮のだし汁にする。
2　塩ブリは水で洗い4つに切る。さといもとにんじんは皮をむき,やわらかく下ゆでしておく。しいたけは水で戻す。カツオ菜は塩ゆでし,水気をしぼり3cm長さに切っておく。かまぼこは8切れに切る。
3　カツオ菜を除く2の材料を1人前ずつ竹串に色どりよく刺す(こうしておくと具が壊れにくく,盛りやすい)。
4　鍋に1のだしを入れ,串に刺した具を入れてブリに火が通るまで2〜3分煮て調味Aを加える。
5　だしに使った昆布を鍋に敷き,一度水洗いして粉を落としたもちを入れ,水から中火でゆでる。
6　椀にもちを入れ,その上に串から抜いた具を並べ,汁にくぐらせて温めたカツオ菜を盛り,熱い汁を注ぐ。吸い口に松葉ゆずをそえると風味もよい。

[Ingredients]　4 servings
4 round-shaped rice cakes (small-size)
120 g salted *buri* (adult yellowtail)
2 taro potatoes (about 50g/each)
40 g carrots
4 dried *shiitake* mushrooms
150 g *katsuona* leaves
1/2 *itatsuki-kamaboko* (fish paste on a wooden plate)
Ago dashi stock　1200 cc Water
　　　　　　　　7 g dried bonito
　　　　　　　　3 *yakiago* (dried frying fish)
　　　　　　　　1 dried *konbu* kelp 10 cm square (10 g)
Seasoning (A)　5 g salt
　　　　　　　8 cc *sake*
　　　　　　　8 cc *koikuchi* (strong) soy sauce
1/4 *yuzu* citrus fruit
4 bamboo skewers

[Directions]
1　[How to prepare *dashi* stock for *zoni*] Pinch away or remove entrails of *yakiago* and tear into pieces. Fill a pot with cold water, and add *konbu* kelp and *yakiago*. Place the pot over heat and just before boiling, remove the kelp from the pot. Reduce the heat to simmer for 5-6 minutes, add dried bonito, simmer for 1 minute, and turn off the heat. Let stand for 5 minutes and strain soup.
2　Cut salted *buri* into 4 pieces. Peel taro potatoes and carrots, and boil them until tender. Soak dried *shiitake* mushrooms in warm water to reconstitute. Boil *katsuona* leaves in lightly salted water, wring dry, and cut into 3 cm lengths. Slice *kamaboko* into 8 pieces.
3　Skewer all ingredients except for *katsuona* with bamboo skewers for individual servings. By skewering, you can ensure that each serving will keep its shape while simmering and serve easily.
4　Pour 1 into the pan, add the skewers, and heat for a few minutes until yellowtails are tender. Add Seasoning (A).
5　Place the used *konbu* kelp at the bottom of a pot. Wash the powder off *mochi* cakes, add to the pot with cold water, and boil at medium temperature.
6　Place the boiled rice cake (5) in individual bowls for serving. Soak *katsuona* in the *dashi* stock to warm. Pull ingredients off skewers and arrange in bowls with the *katsuona,* and then pour in *dashi* stock. Garnish with sliced *yuzu,* if desired.

がめ煮（筑前煮）*Game-ni / Chikuzen-ni*

Boiled Chicken and Vegetables

E 278 kcal／DF 3.1 g／S 1.8 g （1人分　1 serving）

[材料]　4人分
鶏骨つき肉　300 g
さといも　200 g
にんじん　70 g
たけのこ　80 g
干ししいたけ　10 g（3，4枚）
こんにゃく　80 g
絹さや　5枚
だし　400cc
濃口醤油　25cc（大さじ 1 2/3）
塩　3 g（小さじ1/2）
みりん　30cc（大さじ 2）
砂糖　30 g（大さじ 3）
サラダ油　15cc（大さじ 1）

[作り方]
1　鶏肉はひと口大に切る。
2　さといもは皮をむいて乱切りにし，塩でもんで水洗いしてゆがく（後でもう一度煮るので，ここでは中まで完全に火を通す必要はない）。
3　にんじん，たけのこは乱切り，こんにゃくはスプーンでちぎるように切り 2〜3分ゆでてザルにとる。しいたけは戻して銀杏切り，絹さやはすじをとりさっとゆでて水にとる。
4　鍋に油を熱し，鶏肉を入れて軽く炒め，にんじん，たけのこ，しいたけ，こんにゃくを入れてさらに炒め，だしを加えて 2分間煮る。次に砂糖を加え 2分間煮てから塩を入れ，煮汁が半量になったら醤油，みりん，さといもを加えて汁気がなくなるくらいまでゆっくり味を染み込ませるように煮る。
5　器に盛り，絹さやを飾る。

[Ingredients] 4 servings
300 g boney chicken
200 g taro potatoes
70 g carrots
80 g bamboo shoots
3-4 dried *shiitake* mushrooms
  (10 g)
80 g cake devil's tongue
5 snow peas
400 cc *dashi* stock
25 cc *koikuchi* (strong)
  soy sauce
3g salt
30 cc *mirin*
  (sweet cooking *sake*)
30 g sugar
15 cc cooking oil

[Directions]
1　Chop chicken into bite-sized pieces.
2　Peel taro potatoes, chop into chunks, rub with salt, wash off salt, and parboil. Soak dried *shiitake* mushrooms in warm water to reconstitute, and cut into half-moons.
3　Chop carrots and bamboo shoots into chunks. Tear devil's tongue apart with spoon. Boil the devil's tongue for a few minutes and drain with a sieve. Soak the dried *shiitake* mushrooms in water to soften, and cut into quarter-rounds. Remove the strings of the snow peas, boil briefly in water mixed with a pinch of salt, and rinse in cold water.
4　Heat the cooking oil in a pot, add the chicken, and fry lightly. Add the carrots, bamboo shoots, *shiitake* mushrooms and devil's tongue, and continue to fry. Pour in *dashi* stock and simmer for 2 minutes. Add sugar and continue to simmer for 2 minutes, and then add salt. When the liquid reduces to half, add the soy sauce, *mirin* sweet cooking *sake,* and taro potatoes, and continue to simmer until dry to ensure that all the ingredients are seasoned thoroughly.
5　Serve with snow peas.

がめ煮の話　福岡の代表的な郷土料理で，いろいろな材料をがめくりこんで煮る（「がめくりこむ」とは博多の方言で，自分の手もとに多くのものを寄せ集めるという意味がある）ことに由来する。また昔，博多湾河口近くのどぶがめやどろがめ（スッポン）を煮た「かめ煮」が始まりで，江戸後期に鶏肉を使うようになったともいわれる。海に近いところでは鶏肉の代わりにサワラが使われる。福岡以外の地方では筑前煮（筑前国の煮物），いり鶏（炒めてから煮る）と呼ばれている。博多では，正月や祭りには必ずといっていいほど作られ，県全域で同じようなものが作られる。

Gameni　*Gameni* is a local Hakata specialty signature dish. The name is said to originate from the preparation of the dish: *Gamekurikomu* (Hakata dialect meaning "bring together") and *niru* (boil). It is also said that in old times *dobugame* or *dorogame* (snapping turtles), which could be found around the Hakata-wan bay, were used in this dish and that it was in the late Edo Period that chicken came to be used instead. Since Fukuoka is near the sea, Spanish mackerel is sometimes substituted for chicken. In other regions, this dish is called "*Chikuzenni*" (a boiled dish of Chikuzen Province), or "*Iridori*" (fry before boiling). In Fukuoka, *Gameni* is almost always made at New Years and during festivals, with basically the same dish being made throughout the entire prefecture.

Column

博多の屋台

福岡を訪れたら，多くの屋台を目にすることができる。焼き鳥，天ぷら，ラーメン，おでん，そして，ときには餃子などの中華風のものまで，屋台にはいろいろな食べ物が並ぶ。地方によっても内容が異なり，北九州市の屋台ではアルコール類は出さないが，おはぎが置いてある。

屋台では長いすに座って，食事を楽しみながら，他のお客と言葉を交わそう。どの屋台でも，ビール，日本酒，焼酎など，さまざまな種類のアルコールを出す。

おそらく，外国人に一番人気があるのは焼き鳥を出す屋台だろう。焼き鳥のメニューには文字どおりの鶏肉だけでなく，牛肉，豚肉，野菜，魚介類などもある。

海外からの旅行者であっても，屋台を試してみるのに心配は無用だ。屋台の店主は親切だし，日本には厳しい食品衛生法があるから，屋台での食事はいつでも，楽しくて安心だ。

Yatai in Fukuoka

You can find many street food stalls called "*yatai*" in Fukuoka. There are *yatai* selling *yakitori, tempura, ramen, oden* and even some serving *gyoza* and other Chinese food. Dishes served at *yatai* also vary by location. In Kitakyushu City alcoholic drinks are not on the menu, but *ohagi* (a rice ball coated with sweetened red beans) is served.

In every *yatai* there is a bench you can sit on, and you can share a conversation with other customers while enjoying the food. All serve different kinds of alcohol like beer, *sake* and *shochu* (a kind of distilled spirit).

Probably the most popular kind of *yatai* with non-Japanese is the *yakitori yatai*. *Yakitori* is literally grilled chicken but there many other kinds of grilled dishes such as beef, pork, vegetables and seafood.

The overseas visitor does not have to feel so nervous about trying out a *yatai*. The owners are friendly and there are strict health and hygiene laws which ensure that the food is always safe.

お菓子
Sweets

承天寺
Jotenji Temple
（写真提供＝福岡市）

酒饅頭 *Sake Manju*　　　E 179 kcal ／ DF 2.2 g ／ S － (1個分　1 bun)
Sake Buns

酒饅頭の話　博多の名刹・承天寺（福岡市博多区）の開山として知られる鎌倉時代の
僧・聖一国師（円爾弁円）。彼は，留学先である宋（中国）の饅頭の製法を博多商人・
栗波吉右衛門に伝授した。吉右衛門はその製法をもとに，甘酒をしぼってモチ米の粉を
加え発酵させ，その中に餡を入れて蒸し上げ，それを竹の皮で包んだ甘酒饅頭を作った。
これが日本の饅頭の始まりといわれている。

Sake Manju　Shoichi Kokushi (Enni Ben'en), a Buddhist priest from the
Kamakura Era and founder of one of Hakata's noted temples, Jotenji, learned
the recipe for *manju* while studying in Sung China and passed it on to Hakata
merchant Kuriha Kichiemen. Kichiemen took the recipe and added *sake* and
mochi flour to make *Sake Manju*. The mixture was left to rise and bean paste
was added before steaming. After steaming, the *manju* was wrapped in a bamboo leaf. This is said to be the origin of *manju* in Japan.

[材料] 12個分
大和芋　60g
砂糖　200g
酒かす　60g
酒　50cc
小麦粉　200g
ベーキングパウダー　4g（小さじ1）
小豆餡（こしあん，市販品）　240g

[作り方]
1　小豆餡は，12個に分け丸めておく。
2　ボールに酒かすを入れ，酒を少しずつ加え，よくまぜ合わせたら空気が入らないようにラップをし，常温（温かい場所）に50分間置く。
3　大和芋の皮をむき，すり鉢ですりおろし，さらに，すりこ木でまぜる。砂糖を数回に分けて加え，さらにまぜる。
4　2を3に2～3回に分けてまぜる。
5　小麦粉とベーキングパウダーを4に入れ，手でもみ込むようにして，耳たぶくらいの固さにし，まんじゅうの皮を作る。
6　5を12個に分け，中に1を入れて包み，丸く形を整える。
7　布巾を敷いた蒸し器に6を入れ，強火で15～20分間蒸す。
8　蒸し上がったら火からおろし，手早くうちわであおいで照りを出す。

[Ingredients] makes 12
60 g *yamato imo* potatoes
200 g sugar
60 g *sakekasu* (sake lees)
50 cc *sake*
200 g wheat flour
4 g baking powder
240 g *koshian* (strained red bean) paste *commercially available

[Directions]
1　Form the red bean paste into 12 rounds.
2　Put the sake lees in a bowl, add *sake* gradually in small amounts, and mix well. Wrap the mixture after mixing, being careful not to allow any air in, and leave at room temperature (in a warm place) for 50 mins.
3　Peel the potatoes, mash in a grinding bowl, and mix with a wooden pestle. Add sugar in several parts and mix.
4　Add 2 to 3 in 2 or 3 parts while mixing.
5　[To make the *manju* dough] Add flour and baking powder to 4, rub the mixture together by hand until soft.
6　Divide 5 in 12 pieces, fill with 1 and form into rounds.
7　Place 6 in a steam cooker lined with a cloth and steam for 15-20 mins.
8　Remove from heat and quickly fan the *manju* to glaze.

博多水無月 *Hakata Minazuki*
Hakata Bean Dumplings

E 68 kcal ／ DF 9.3 g ／ S － （1 個分 1 dumpling）

[材料] 10個分
わらび粉 150 g
水 500cc
砂糖 50 g
ゆで小豆（市販品） 50 g

[作り方]
1 鍋にわらび粉，水，砂糖を入れてよくまぜ，中火にかけて木杓子で絶えずまぜながら火を通す。全体が透き通った状態になったら，火からおろす。
2 1の中にゆで小豆をまぜ，粗熱をとり，10個に丸める。
3 2を笹の葉にくるみ，器に盛る。

[Ingredients] makes 10
150 g *warabi* (bracken starch) flour
500 cc water
50 g sugar
50 g boiled *azuki* beans
　*commercially available

[Directions]
1 Put bracken starch, water and sugar into a pot and mix well. Heat over medium temperature while stirring constantly with a wooden spatula. When the mixture is transparent, remove from heat.
2 Mix the *azuki* beans with 1, and form into 10 rounds when cool enough to touch.
3 Wrap in a bamboo leaf and arrange in a dish.

博多水無月の話　昔から，1年のちょうど半分にあたる6月30日（晦日）を無事に越えればその1年を平穏に過ごせるということで，この日に水無月（和菓子）を食べて邪気を払うという「水無月祓い」が全国各地で行われる。博多水無月は「あずきとわらび粉を主原料とし，笹で巻く」ことを決まり事としている。

Hakata Minazuki　From olden times it has been said that if we manage to get through the first half of the year without incident, we will be able to pass the whole year peacefully. So on June 30th all over Japan, a summer purification ritual was held and *Minazuki* was eaten to ward off bad spirits. *Hakata Minazuki* is known for being made of *azuki* and bracken starch, and for being wrapped in a bamboo leaf.

鶏卵素麺 *Keiran Somen*

Angel Hair *Keiran Somen*

E 153 kcal ／ DF － ／ S 0.2 g

[材料] 5人分
卵 10個
白双糖(しろざらとう) 200 g
水 100cc
ビニール袋 1枚

[作り方]
1 卵を割り，卵黄のみを布ごしする。
2 2個分の卵白を軽く泡立てる。
3 1の卵黄の中へ2の卵白を入れ，まぜながら4～5分湯煎にかける。
4 鍋に水と白双糖を入れて火にかけ，少し糸を引く程度(110℃)まで煮詰める。
5 ビニール袋に3を入れ，そそぎ口を作る。
6 4の中に円を描くように5を流し込み，2～3分煮てとり出し，少し冷まして器に盛る。

鶏卵素麺の話　鶏卵素麺のルーツは，ポルトガルのサン・レアンドゥロ修道院の修道女たちが作るイェマス・デ・サン・レアンドゥロという菓子である。これを日本で初めて本格的に製造したとされるのが，博多の老舗菓子店・松屋の初代・松屋利右衛門。延宝年間(1673～81年)，利右衛門は博多の豪商・大賀家の縁故により，中国人の鄭氏から伝授されたという。その製法は一子相伝で，日本三大銘菓の1つにも数えられる。

[Ingredients] 5 servings
10 eggs
200 g confectioners' sugar
100 cc water
1 pastry bag

[Directions]
1　Break the eggs and strain the yolks through a cloth.
2　Lightly beat the whites of 2 eggs.
3　Pour the egg whites (1) into the yolks (2) and warm the dish in a pot containing water while stirring for 4-5 mins.
4　Put water and confectioners' sugar in a pot and boil to 110℃ until slightly sticky.
5　Pour 3 into the pastry bag and form a spout.
6　Pour 5 into 4 in a circular motion, heat for 2-3 mins, and leave to cool slightly before putting in a dish.

Angel Hair *Keiran Somen*　The recipe for Angel Hair *Keiran Somen* comes from a sweet called Yemas de San Leandro, made by the sisters of the Portuguese convent San Leandro. It was first produced on a large scale in Japan by Matsuya Riemon, the founder of Hakata's well-established Matsuya. Riemon was taught the recipe during the Empou Era (1673-1681) by a Mr. Zheng, a Chinese acquaintance made through Hakata's wealthy merchant Ogha family. The recipe for Angel Hair *Keiran Somen* is handed down in the family through only one son. It is counted as one of the 3 top confections in Japan.

くずもち *Kuzu mochi*

Kuzu Mochi with a Sweet Topping

E 232 kcal ／ DF 1.2 g ／ S 0.1 g （1人分　1 serving）

くずもちの話　本くず粉の原料は寒根（かんね）かずらの根からとったデンプンである。「秋月くず」は秋月藩御用達の伝統的な特産品で，江戸時代には幕府へ献上されていた。くずには風邪や下痢止めなどの薬効があるといわれ，くず湯がよく飲まれていた。現在はくず饅頭やくず切りなどの和菓子や料理のトロミづけとして使われている。

Kuzu mochi　The material of "*Hon-kuzu*" powder is starch flour taken from *Kan'ne* vines. *Akizuki Kuzu* is a signature agricultural product, produced under an Akizuki clan warrant, which was presented to the Edo Shogunate. It is believed that *Kuzu* has medicinal properties which help to relieve colds, diarrhea, and other maladies, so *Kuzu* is widely taken together with hot water. *Kuzu* is often used as an ingredient for sweets, like *Kuzu Manju* buns or *Kuzu-kiri* sliced sweets, or for adding thickness to foods.

[材料] 4人分
本くず粉　150g
水　600cc
砂糖　50g
きな粉
　きな粉　30g（大さじ3）
　砂糖　30g（大さじ3）
　塩　ひとつまみ
黒みつ
　黒砂糖　100g
　水　100cc
　卵白　1/2個分

[作り方]
1　鍋にくず粉，水，砂糖を入れてよく
まぜ，くず粉を完全にとかす。
2　1を中火にかけ，木杓子で絶えずま
ぜながら火を通す。鍋底からプクプクと
くず粉がふくれあがり全体が透き通った
状態になったら流し箱に入れ，氷水で粗
熱をとり，さらに冷蔵庫で冷やし固める。
3　きな粉の材料をまぜ合わせる。
4　黒みつを作る。鍋に黒砂糖，水，卵
白を入れてよくまぜ，強火にかけ木杓子
で鍋底から絶えずまぜ続ける。沸騰直前
になったらまぜるのをやめ，コトコト煮
立つぐらいの火で5分間煮て布ごしをす
る。さらに2分の1〜3分の1の量にな
るまで煮つめてから冷やす。
5　2のくずもちをとり出して好みの大
きさに切り，きな粉と黒みつをかけて食
べる。

[Ingredients]　4 servings
150 g *kuzu* powder
600 cc water
50 g sugar
Kinako topping
　30 g *kinako* (soybean flour)
　30 g sugar
　Pinch salt
Kuromitsu topping
　100 g unrefined sugar
　100 cc water
　1/2 egg white

[Directions]
1　Pour *kuzu* powder, water, and sugar into a pot and stir until the powder is fully dissolved.
2　Simmer over medium heat while stirring with a wooden spatula. When the mixture puffs up from the bottom of the pot and turns transparent, pour into a mold pan, and cool the pan in iced water. Refrigerate to set.
3　[How to prepare *kinako* topping] Mix *kinako* with sugar and salt.
4　[How to prepare *kuromitsu* topping] Mix refined sugar, water and egg white in a pot, place over high heat, and keep mixing from the bottom of the pot with a wooden spatula. Just before boiling, stop mixing, simmer for 5 minutes, and then strain the liquid through a kitchen towel. Boil down the strained liquid until reduced by half to one third, and let stand to cool.
5　Take the *kuzumochi* jelly out of the mold pan (2), and cut into any size you like. Serve with *kinako* topping and *kuromitsu* topping.

ふなやき *Funayaki*　E 89 kcal ／ DF 1.7 g ／ S 0.2 g　（1人分　1 serving）
Crepe à la Fukuoka

[材料]　4人分
薄力粉　50 g
水または牛乳　120cc
塩　ひとつまみ
しその葉　5枚
黒砂糖　80 g
サラダ油　5 cc（小さじ1）

[作り方]
1　ボールに水と塩を入れてまぜ，ふるった薄力粉を少しずつ加えてよくまぜ合わせてからこし，30分間おく。
2　1の中にしその葉の荒みじん切りしたものを加え，テフロン加工のフライパンに油を薄く引き，中火で両面焼く。全体に黒砂糖をふって火を止め，手前から巻く。

[Ingredients]　4 servings
50 g soft flour
120 cc water or milk
1 g salt
5 *shiso*
　(Japanese perilla)
80 g unrefined sugar
5 cc cooking oil

[Directions]
1　Sieve soft flour. Pour water and salt in a bowl, add the flour gradually, mix well, strain, and then leave for 30 minutes.
2　Chop the *shiso* leaves, and add to 1. Fry both sides over medium heat in a lightly oiled Teflon-coated pan, sprinkle on unrefined sugar, and turn off the heat. Fold up like a crepe.

ふなやきの話　福岡県内で一番大きな筑後川では，昔は船を使っての人や物資の運搬が盛んであった。この船で仕事をしている人たちが，午後3時頃になると少しお腹がすいてくるため，船の上で七輪を用意し，鉄板をかけ，ふなやきを作っておやつとして食べていた。

Funayaki　Chikugogawa, the largest river in Fukuoka prefecture, once thrived on the transportation of people and goods by ship. The workers on the ships used to take an afternoon snack break at around 3 pm. They set up *shichirin* (a charcoal stove) with an iron plate on their ship and enjoyed *Funayaki* as a light snack.

ごろし *Goroshi*

Kinako Sweets

E 199 kcal ／ DF 7.7 g ／ S 0.2 g
（1 人分　1 serving）

[材料]　4 人分
薄力粉　50 g
強力粉　50 g
塩　ひとつまみ
水　60cc
（別に）
　黒砂糖　30 g（大さじ 3）
　きな粉　きな粉　30 g（大さじ 3）
　　　　　砂糖　30 g（大さじ 3）
　　　　　塩　ひとつまみ

[作り方]
1　ボールにふるった薄力粉，強力粉，塩，水を加え木杓子でまぜる。次に手でよくこね，1 つにまとまったらぬれ布巾に包み 1 時間ぐらいおいておく。
2　1 をさらにこね，表面がなめらかになったら 3 ㎝ぐらいの団子を作り，両手で薄く引きのばしてからたっぷりの湯でゆでる。
3　2 が上に浮き上がってきたら火を止め，鍋ぶたをして 2〜3 分蒸らしザルにとる。
4　きな粉の材料をまぜ合わせる。
5　器に 3 をおき黒砂糖やきな粉をかけて食べる。

ごろしの話　今のように甘いお菓子を簡単に買うことができなかった頃は，手軽にこういうものを作りおやつとして食べていた。白い小麦粉のだごが黒砂糖の色で殺されるということで「ごろし」，また五郎次という人が作り始めたという説もある。包丁で切ったものは「切りごろし」，ゆで上がっただごを油で炒めたものを「あぶらげごろし」ともいう。

[Ingredients]　4 servings
50 g soft flour
50 g strong flour
Pinch salt
60 cc water
(Topping)
　30 g unrefined sugar
　Kinako topping　30 g *kinako* (soybean flour)
　　　　　　　　　　30 g sugar
　　　　　　　　　　Pinch salt

[Directions]
1　Sieve soft flour and strong flour. Pour the flour, salt, and water into a bowl, and mix with a wooden spatula. Knead dough thoroughly by hand and cover with a wet cloth to let rest for 1 hour.
2　Knead the dough again until the surface is smooth. Roll into 3 cm-sized balled dumplings and spread thinly with your hands. Boil in a pot filled with hot water.
3　When the dumplings rise to the surface of the water, turn off the heat, and cover the pot with a lid. Wait for a few minutes, then remove and drain with a sieve.
4　[How to prepare *kinako* topping] Mix *kinako* with sugar and salt.
5　Place the dumplings on individual plates, and serve with unrefined sugar and *kinako* topping.

Goroshi　People in old times, unlike us, couldn't afford to buy snacks easily. Instead, they often cooked and ate simple sweets. There are two explanations regarding the origin of "*goroshi*". One theory says that a man named "*goroji*" was the first inventor. The other says that the white color of dumpling is "killed" (destroyed) or "*korosu*" by the blackish color of the brown sugar. "*kiri-goroshi*" (sliced goroshi) and "*aburage-goroshi*" (boiled and fried *goroshi*) are two variations on this dish.

さんきら饅頭（がめの葉饅頭）

Sankira Manju (Gamenoha Manju)

Catbrier Buns

E 92 kcal ／ DF 1.5 g ／ S － （1個分　1 bun）

[材料] 12個分
上新粉　200g
ぬるま湯　160cc
塩　ひとつまみ
片栗粉　9g（大さじ1）
小豆餡（こしあん，市販品）　240g
さんきらの葉　24枚

[Ingredients] makes 12
200 g *joshinko* (top-grade rice flour)
160 cc lukewarm water
pinch salt
1 tbsp *katakuriko* (potato starch) 9 g
240 g *koshian azuki* paste
    *commercially available
24 *sankira* (catbrier) leaves

[作り方]
1　ボールに上新粉とひとつまみの塩を入れて，ぬるま湯で練り，片栗粉を入れてさらにまぜる。
2　布巾を敷いた蒸し器に1を入れ，強火で20分程度蒸し，一度とり出し熱いうちによくこねる。餅状になったら12個に分けておく。
3　小豆餡を12個に丸め，2の皮で包み，さんきら（がめ）の葉ではさみ，強火で8分程度蒸し，器に盛る。

[Directions]
1　Put rice flour and salt in a bowl and soften with lukewarm water. Add potato starch and mix.
2　Put 1 in a steamer lined with a cloth and steam for 20 mins. Remove and knead while hot. When it reaches the consistency of *mochi*, divide into 12.
3　Form the *azuki* paste into 12 rounds. Cover with the dough and wrap in a catbrier leaf. Steam for approximately 8 minutes and arrange in a dish.

さんきら饅頭の話　「さんきら」は「山帰来」と書き，サルトリイバラのこと。葉の見た目がカメの甲羅に似ていることから，「がめの葉」とも呼ばれる。饅頭を葉で包むことで，蒸し上がったときに独特の香りがつく。筑前・筑後地方でよく作られ，端午の節句や夏祭り，お盆，法事などに食べられた。

Sankira Mochi　*Sankira* refers to catbrier and is sometimes called tortoise leaf because it looks like a tortoise shell. Steaming the *manju* in this leaf gives it a special aroma. It was often made in the Chikuzen and Chikugo regions and eaten on Boy's Day, during Obon vacation and summer festivals, and at Buddhist memorial services.

シュガーロード ―― 長崎街道

江戸時代の鎖国政策の下，海外への唯一の窓口であった出島。そこから荷揚げされた砂糖は，長崎から佐賀，福岡を経て小倉へと続く長崎街道を通り，京，大坂，江戸へと運ばれた。長崎街道が「シュガーロード（砂糖の道）」と呼ばれる所以だ。長崎街道は，九州の諸大名の参勤交代の道であるとともに，オランダや中国の異文化を運ぶルートでもあった。

街道沿いの町では，砂糖をはじめとする材料や菓子作りの技法も入手しやすかったことから，様々な菓子が生まれていった。現在でも，寛永元（1624）年創業で長崎カステラの元祖といわれる「福砂屋」のカステラや，文亀2（1502）年創業で平戸藩主・松浦家の御用菓子司だった「蔦屋」のカスドース，元禄9（1696）年に数珠屋として佐賀城下中町に創業した「北島」の丸ぼうろ，そして本文中でも紹介した鶏卵素麺など，全国的に有名な銘菓が残っている。

時が流れ，時代の波にのまれながらも脈々と受け継がれてきた創業者や職人の技と心は，今も確かに息づいている。

Sugar Road ―― Nagasaki Kaido Road

Under the isolation policy of the Edo era, the trading outpost Dejima in Nagasaki was the only entrance to the outside world. Sugar unloaded here followed Nagasaki Kaido Road through Nagasaki, Saga and Fukuoka as far as Kokura, before moving on to Kyoto, Osaka, and finally Edo. This is the reason Nagasaki Kaido Road was called "Sugar Road". Nagasaki Kaido Road was not only the road that the feudal lord of each Daimyo followed on their mandated trip to Edo each year, but also a road transporting the foreign cultures of Holland and China.

Because it was easy for towns along the Kaido Road to gain access to sugar and cooking techniques, a variety of sweets came into being and many of them still exist today. There is the *Castella* of Fukusaya, founded in 1624, which is said to be the original *Castella*; *Casdoce* from Tsutaya, founded in 1502 and patronized by the feudal lord of the Matsura domain; *Maruboro* from Kitajima, founded in Nakamachi Saga Castle Town in 1696 under the name "Juzuya"; and Angel Hair *Keiran Somen*, the recipe for which is introduced in this book. These sweets are famous all over Japan.

Time goes by and we get swept along with the winds of change, but the techniques and hearts of the founder and artisans of these confections continue to be handed down, still breathing life into their creation today.

長崎街道　Nagasaki Kaido Road
＊主な宿場町のみ表示　Only major post towns shown

黒崎 Kurosaki	小倉 Kokura
	木屋瀬 Koyanose
原田 Harada	内野 Uchino
塩田 Shiota	佐賀 Saga
嬉野 Ureshino	大村 Omura
長崎 Nagasaki	日見 Himi

食べにきんしゃい
Come and Dine!

柳橋連合市場
Yanagibashi-rengo Market

焼きガキ
Baked Oysters

福岡県の沿岸部ではカキの養殖をしているところが多いが，その中でも「糸島カキロード」といわれる福吉，深江，加布里（かふり），船越，岐志新町（きししんまち），野北（のぎた）の各漁港周辺，「唐泊（からどまり）恵比須カキ」の福岡市西区唐泊，「豊前一粒カキ」の行橋市蓑島（みのしま）や豊前市近辺などがよく知られている。11月中旬から2月くらいの時期には，各漁港周辺の店（カキ小屋）で焼きガキを食べることができる。

The coastal area of Fukuoka has many oyster farms, particularly at the fishing ports along the so-called "Itoshima Oyster Road", including Fukuyoshi, Fukae, Kafuri, Funakoshi, Kishishinmachi, and Nogita. Karadomari, Nishi Ward in Fukuoka City, produces brand-name oysters under the name "*Karadomari Ebisu Kaki*", and Minoshima in Yukuhashi City and the vicinity of Buzen City under "*Buzen Hitotsubu Kaki*". You can enjoy baked oysters at shops in each fishing port during the season from mid-November to February.

大勢の人で賑わう唐泊のカキ小屋。自ら焼くのも楽しい（写真提供＝福岡市漁協唐泊支所）

釣りあじ玄ちゃんの活造り

Fresh Slices of "*Tsuri* (fishing)-*Aji* (mackerel)- *Genchan*"

鐘崎(かねざき)漁協釣りアジ船団が大島と地島(じのしま)周辺海域で一本釣りした瀬付きのアジのうち，頭から尻尾の付け根までの長さが26cm以上のものを「釣りあじ玄ちゃん」のブランド名で売り出している。絶対に手で触らないようにし，鮮度を管理・保持して出荷している。活造りは鐘崎，神湊(こうのみなと)の宿泊施設及び飲食店で1年中食べることができるが，冬季は時化(しけ)が多く漁獲量が激減する。おいしいのは6月から9月の脂ののった時期である。

(写真提供＝鐘崎漁協)

Kanezaki Fishermen's Cooperative Association Horse Mackerel Fishing Fleet does "*ippon-zuri*" (pole-and-line) fishing in the sea around Jinoshima and Oshima. Horse mackerel with dorsal fins, and over 26 cms in length from the head to the root of the caudal fin, are labeled "*Tsuri* (fishing) -*Aji* (mackerel) - *Genchan*". To ensure the freshness of the fish, the fishermen are careful to avoid touching it with their nets or hands. You can taste this fish at accomodations and restaurants in Kanezaki and Kounominato all year round, although fish catches tend to decrease due to storms in winter. Horse mackerel is especially good to eat from June to September, when it is rich in fat.

あしやんいかの活造り

Fresh Slices of *Ashiyan Ika* Squid

玄界灘の芦屋沖で一本釣りされるヤリイカ（地方によってはケンサキイカともいう）にこのブランド名がつけられている。釣り上がったものは，手で触らずそのまま生けすに入れて運んでくる。1年中とれるが，5〜11月の間が漁獲量も多く，まるまると肥えたヤリイカが食べられる。生きたままを手早く刺身にするため，身は透明で，コリコリした歯ざわりの中にもやわらかくて甘みがある。足の部分は生で食べてもおいしいが，天ぷらや塩焼きにもしてくれる。筑前あしや海の駅や周辺の料理屋で食べることができる。

透明な身の刺身は，コリコリした食感と
甘味が特長（写真提供＝遠賀漁協）

Ashiyan Ika is speared squid (*Yariika/Kensaki ika*) and is caught offshore of Ashiya, Genkai Nada. After being caught, it is carried live in an *ikesu,* a fishing reserve, without being touched by hand. Squid is caught all year round, with the period from May to November being the peak season, when you can enjoy the richest taste of the squid. As it is prepared quickly as *sashimi* and served live, the meat is translucent and crunchy but still tender, and has a certain sweetness. Squid tentacles are also very delicious raw, but you can ask for them to be to cooked as *tempura* or *shioyaki* (lightly salted and baked). *Ashiyan Ika* is served at Chikuzen-Ashiya-Umi-no-Eki Station and at nearby restaurants.

ウナギの蒸籠蒸し

Eels Steamed in a Basket

ウナギは，江戸時代後期ごろに
は蒲（かば）焼きとして庶民の間
で食べられていた。柳川の蒸籠
（せいろ）蒸しは，背開きしたウ
ナギを串に刺さずに白焼きした
後，タレを 2〜3 回つけて焼き，
タレをまぶした蒸しご飯の上に
のせ，錦糸卵をのせてさらに蒸
し上げる。ご飯にもタレがしみ
込み，やわらかいウナギととも
に食べる味は独特のおいしさで
ある。ちなみに粉さんしょうは
使わない。

（写真提供＝柳川市）

Eel has been eaten as "broiled eel" or *kabayaki* as early as the late Edo era.
"Steamed eel à la Yanagawa" is prepared by first preparing eel fillets opened
along the spine, and grilling them without skewering. Sauce is then spread over
the fillets and they are grilled again. This process is repeated several times. The
fillets are then placed on steamed rice, and shredded thin omelet is sprinkled on
top. They are again steamed. By following this process, sauce sinks into the
rice. This dish is called "Yanaga-no-seiro-mushi" or eel steamed in a basket à
la Yanagawa, and its taste of rice with tender eel is absolutely delicious. Inciden-
tally, *sansho* powder is not used for eel steamed in a basket à la Yanagawa.

幻の魚・エツ

Etsu (Japanese Grenadier Anchovy), an Endangered Fish

塩焼きや天ぷら，煮つ
けなどのエツ料理

全国でも筑後川河口域にしか生息しないとされるエツ。ニシン目カタクチイワシ科で，
銀白色に輝く身の薄い魚である。鮮度が落ちるのが早く，小骨が多くて細かい骨切りが
必要である。その昔，弘法大師が船に乗せてもらったお礼に川に投げ入れた葦（よし）の
葉がエツになったという伝説がある。有明海から産卵のため川を上がってくる5月1日
〜7月20日前後が漁の解禁日となっており，周辺の料理店や屋形船で食べることができ
る。年々漁獲量が少なくなっていて，まさに幻の魚となるかもしれない。

Etsu is a fish said to only inhabit the mouth of the Chikugogawa River and is
classified by the Latin name of Clupeiformes (from the family of fish called
Engraulidae). It has a thin body and a silvery glitter, and after being caught,
loses its freshness easily. It is full of fine bones, so the bones need to be removed when cooking. A local legend has it that a famous Japanese monk
called Kobo Daishi/Kukai, as a token of his thanks for a boat ride, threw reed
leaves into Chikugogawa River, and the leaves turned into *etsu* fish. The *etsu*
season opens from around May 1st to July 20th, when the fish goes up river to
spawn from the Ariake Sea. During this season, you can eat *etsu* at restaurants or on *yakatabune* houseboats near the river. As the catches have been
decreasing year by year, *etsu* may become extinct someday.

フルーツ狩り
Fruit Picking

福岡では県下全域で，四季折々に旬のフルーツ狩りを楽しむことができる。主なものでは，いちご狩り（12〜5月），ぶどう狩り（8〜9月），なし狩り（8〜10月），かき狩り（10〜11月）があり，その他にも，ブルーベリー，いちじく，りんご，みかん，キウイなど多くのフルーツ狩りが行われている。

（写真提供＝上は久留米市，他は福岡県農産物ブランド化推進協議会）

You can enjoy seasonal fruit picking across Fukuoka Prefecture. There are strawberries (December to May), grapes (August to September), pears (August to October) and persimmons (October to November). Various other kinds of fruit can be picked in Fukuoka Prefecture, including peaches, blueberries, figs, apples, tangerines, and kiwi fruits.

食べにきんしゃい Come and Dine!　93

調理・食材単語リスト Glossary

調理の動作
Verbs for Cooking

アクをとる　skim off foam
うろこを落とす　scale
おろす（おろし金などで）　grate
かきまぜる（卵などを）　beat
飾る,つまをあしらう　garnish
皮をむく　peel
切る　cut
切る（乱切りにする,粗く切る）
　　chop
串刺しにする　skewer
加える　add
こす　strain
こねる　knead
冷ます（熱いものを室温まで）
　　cool
ザルにあげる,水気を切る
　　drain with a sieve
炊く,火を通して調理する
　　cook
出す（飲み物,食べ物を）　serve
とりのぞく　remove
煮る（沸騰させる）　boil
煮る（弱火でコトコト）　simmer
ひたす　soak
ふたをする　cover
ふりかける,ちらす　sprinkle
水洗いする,すすぐ　rinse
盛りつける　arrange
ゆがく,湯通しする　parboil

調理道具
Cooking Utensils

おたま　ladle
落としぶた　drop-lid
木杓子　wooden spatula
ザル　sieve
すし桶　wooden sushi bowl
すりこぎ　pestle

すりばち　grinding bowl
竹串　bamboo skewer
土鍋　earthen pot
流し型　mold pan
鍋　pot
布巾　cloth
フライパン　frying pan
包丁　knife
まな板　cutting board
ラップ　plastic wrap/cling film

調味料
Spices

薄口醤油　light soy sauce
黒砂糖　unrefined sugar
濃口醤油　strong soy sauce
塩　salt
酢　vinegar
赤唐辛子　red pepper
みりん
　　mirin sweet cooking sake

野菜
Vegetables

かいわれ　radish sprout
かんぴょう
　　dried gourd shaving
きくらげ　wood ear
ごぼう　burdock root
こんにゃく　devil's tongue
さといも　taro potato
さやえんどう　snow pea
しそ　Japanese green perilla
春菊
　　Shungiku Chrysanthemum leaf
せり　Japanese parsley
だいこん　Japanese radish
たけのこ　bamboo shoot
つくし　horsetail
にら　Chinese chive
にんじん　carrot

にんにく　garlic
白菜　Chinese cabbage
ふき　Japanese butterbur
三つ葉　Japanese hornwort
もやし　bean sprout
れんこん　lotus root
わけぎ　green onion

魚介類
Fish and Seafood

アサリ貝　shucked littleneck
アジ　horse mackerel
アナゴ　sea eel
あぶってかも（スズメダイ）
　　pearl-spot chromis
イカ　squid
イワシ　sardine
エビ　prawn
カマス　barracuda
くつぞこ　sole
コノシロ　mango fish
サザエ　turban shell
サバ　mackerel
シロウオ　ice goby
タイ　sea-bream
ハマグリ　clam
ブリ　adult yellowtail

その他の食材
Others

いりこ　dried sardine
炒りごま　parched sesame
カツオ節　dried bonito
かまぼこ　fish paste
きな粉　soybean flour
強力粉　strong flour
昆布　konbu kelp
溶き卵　beaten egg
鶏がら　chicken bone
薄力粉　soft flour
わさび　Japanese horseradish

著者略歴 　About Authors

津田晶子　比較社会文化学博士，英語科教授法修士。百道中学校，修猷館高校，九州大学を卒業後，外資系航空会社地上総合職，ビジネス翻訳業を経て大学英語教員に。中村学園大学栄養科学部フード・マネジメント学科准教授。英国レディング大学客員研究員（2013年度）。好きな福岡の食べ物は母の作る博多雑煮とあまおう。ラーメンはバリカタ。

Akiko TSUDA　PhD Cultural Studies, MEd TESOL, Visiting Scholar at University of Reading, UK (April 2013 - March 2014)
A native of Fukuoka, Dr. Tsuda graduated from Kyushu University before going on to work an airline, and as a freelance translator. Currently, she serves as an Associate Professor at Food Management Faculty of Nutritional Sciences, Nakamura Gakuen University. Her Mom's "Hakata Zoni", "Amao ichigo strawberries" and "Very Hard Ramen" are her great favorite.

松隈紀生　管理栄養士，専門調理師（西洋料理）。中村学園大学家政学部管理栄養士専攻を卒業後，イタリア，フランスにて調理研修。元中村学園大学短期大学部食物栄養学科教授。共著に『アクロス福岡文化誌2　ふるさとの食』（海鳥社），『基礎と応用の調理学実習』（講談社）など。料理雑誌での執筆，テレビ出演多数。

Norio MATSUKUMA　National Registered Dietitian, Licenced Cook
After graduating from the Home Economics Department, Nakamura Gakuen University, Professor Matsukuma studied cookery in Italy and France. He was former faculty of the Nutrition Science Department, Nakamura Gakuen Jr. College. He has contributed to numerous cookery magazines and appeared on TV as a cooking teacher.

松隈美紀　学術博士，栄養士，調理師，フードスペシャリスト。百道中学校，中村学園女子高等学校，中村学園大学家政学部食物栄養学科卒業後，中村学園大学家政学部助手，短期大学部食物栄養学科助教，講師を経て現在，中村学園大学栄養科学部フード・マネジメント学科教授として調理学実習を担当。

Miki MATSUGUMA　Ph.D. Dietetics, Licensed Cook, Food Specialist
After studying at Momochi Junior High School, Nakamura Gakuen Girls High School, and graduating from Nakamura Gakuen Junior University's Food and Nutrition Department, she worked as Professor at Food Management Faculty of Nutritional Sciences, Nakamura Gakuen University. She is currently teaching Culinary and Food Coordinating.

ケリー・マクドナルド　比較社会文化学修士。母国カナダのフランス系大学を卒業後，来日し，日本語と日本文化に親しむ。九州大学大学院にて修士号を修め，現在，大学の講師を務めつつ，フリーランスで翻訳も手がける。ベジタリアン歴が長く，和食好き。新鮮な食材や料理のヒントを求め，健康食品店を訪ねる日々。

Kelly MACDONALD　MA Cultural Studies
After graduating from a French university in her native Canada, Kelly moved to Japan to immerse herself in the Japanese language and culture. She holds an MA from Kyushu University and currently works as both university lecturer and freelance translator. A long-time vegetarian and lover of Japanese food, Kelly can often be found shopping for fresh ingredients and getting cooking tips at health food stores around the city.

トーマス・ケイトン　英語教育学修士。英国ドーセット生まれ。ロンドン大学キングスカレッジを卒業し，レディング大学で修士号（TEFL）を取得後，来日。東京での航空会社勤務を経て，現在，福岡在住23年，中村学園大学短期大学部で英語講師を務める。好きな日本料理は寿司と伝統的な鍋料理。

Thomas CATON　MA TEFL
Born in Dorset in the UK. After graduating from King's College, University of London and completing his MA at the University of Reading in the UK, Professor Caton went on to work for an airline in Tokyo. A resident of Fukuoka for 23 years, he currently teaches English at Nakamura Jr. College. His favourite Japanese cuisine includes *sushi* and traditional *nabe* dishes.

料理制作　松隈紀生・松隈美紀

写真撮影　野村一郎（表紙カバー及び本文 P.1, 18, 24, 30, 32, 44, 46, 48, 50, 51, 52, 53, 58, 60, 62, 64, 66, 68, 69, 70, 76, 78, 79, 84）

　　　　　川上信也（P.23, 37, 55, 87）

　　　　　松隈紀生（上記以外でクレジットのない写真）

英語で楽しむ福岡の郷土料理 ［新装版］
Recipes of Fukuoka ［Reprinted］

2020年2月14日　第1刷発行

著　者　津田晶子　松隈紀生　松隈美紀　ケリー・マクドナルド　トーマス・ケイトン

発行者　杉本雅子

発行所　有限会社海鳥社　〒812-0023　福岡市博多区奈良屋町13番4号
　　　　電話092（272）0120　FAX092（272）0121
　　　　http://www.kaichosha-f.co.jp

印刷・製本　大村印刷株式会社

ISBN 978-4-86656-064-9　［定価は表紙カバーに表示］